ALSO BY JEAN HERSEY

The Woman's Day Book of Wildflowers
Flowering Shrubs and Small Trees
Cooking with Herbs
The Shape of a Year
A Sense of Seasons
The Woman's Day Book of House Plants
Wildflowers to Know and Grow
Carefree Gardening
Garden in Your Window
Halfway to Heaven
I Like Gardening

WITH ROBERT HERSEY

Change in the Wind
These Rich Years

BY

Jean Hersey

ILLUSTRATED BY

Fritz Kredel

SIMON AND SCHUSTER • NEW YORK

The
Woman's Day
Book
of
ANNUALS
and
PERENNIALS

Copyright © 1961, 1977 by Fawcett Publications, Inc.
All rights reserved
including the right of reproduction
in whole or in part in any form
Published by Simon and Schuster
A Division of Gulf & Western Corporation
Simon & Schuster Building
Rockefeller Center
1230 Avenue of the Americas
New York, New York 10020
Designed by Edith Fowler
Manufactured in the United States of America

1   2   3   4   5   6   7   8   9   10

Library of Congress Cataloging in Publication Data

Hersey, Jean, date.
   The Woman's day book of annuals and perennials.
   Includes index.

   1. Annuals (Plants)   2. Perennials.   I. Kredel,
Fritz, 1900–1973.   II. Title.   III. Title: Book of
annuals and perennials.
SB422.H47   1977   635.9'31   76-49507
ISBN 0-671-22508-1

For Joan
Who grows flowers
wherever she is

Acknowledgments

In developing this book, many people have come to my aid. I would like to express thanks to Holly and Harvey Woltman for the use of their fine library; to Fritzie Haugland for her tireless enthusiasm, general help, and meticulous typing. Dan Walden's botanical knowledge and his understanding and skillful editing have been invaluable.

Contents

The philosopher's soul dwells in his head.
The poet's soul dwells in his heart;
The singer's soul dwells in his throat. . . .
But the soul of man who lives among flowers
walks hand in hand with eternity.

KAHLIL GIBRAN

Annuals and Perennials

Annuals are quick and sure, giddy and gay, and bright as the sun itself in which they thrive. Annuals are easy for beginners, they continue flowering all summer right up to and even beyond the first frost or two. When winter descends in a swirl and a blizzard, forget them. In the spring, begin over. A few will reseed, but in the main you plan a new pattern, a varied arrangement for your annual area. Annuals come in every rainbow tint; and if you live at the seashore or where there are heavy dews at night, the tones are especially vivid. Annuals are for those who want a garden in a hurry, a garden of sheer joy, with tangled masses of flowers and armfuls of bouquets for the house. Annuals are for those who want constant variety and vibrant colors, those who desire something new and different each summer. Annuals are for the experimenter.

Perennials are the plants that you make friends with and warmly greet each spring, for they return year after year. Under their snug covering of leaves all winter, the plants grow more and longer roots, and in the spring they emerge a little sturdier, a little larger, from a warming soil. You never need to replant perennials except as you wish to add newer varieties. You merely divide them every few years to share with friends and neighbors. Perennials are the garden's backbone. There are some for every location: sun, shade, semishade, rich soil, poor soil—for they are a large and versatile group.

As you travel through these pages into a world of beauty, pick and choose your special colors, your favorite shapes, the blossoms that especially appeal, that you find irresistible. With some of both annuals and perennials you'll have a garden of solid, sound, dependable varieties, and a garden with a flair. Come to think of it, perhaps this is what we want and need, and not only in the garden—balance and flair!

Part One

ONE HUNDRED ANNUALS

1. One Hundred Annuals

LOW

ALYSSUM, SWEET (*Lobularia mari-*▶
tima 'Carpet of Snow'). Mustard
Family
A native of the Mediterranean region.
A must for every annual garden, where
this white variety creates a veritable
carpet of snow for weeks on end.
Flowers abundantly all summer until,
and even after, the first frost or two.
Sow seeds early, as soon as the ground
can be worked. The first tiny attractive
flowers appear in May. Beautiful
ground cover and edging plant. Dwarf
and neat in growing habit.

HEIGHT: 3 to 6 inches.
COLOR: White, violet, pink.
LOCATION: Full sun.
SOIL: Average; any good garden
loam.
PLANTING: Scatter seeds in a row
in the open ground in early spring. No
need to separate or thin young plants.
USES: To edge flower beds or
rock gardens; to cover banks, in window
boxes, between flagstones. Can be
potted in fall and grown on as a house
plant.
FRAGRANT. Like new-mown hay.
CULTURAL HINTS: A couple of
times during the summer when the
plants grow taller and appear to
straggle, shear way back. In two weeks
more flowers will appear.

AFRICAN DAISY (*Arctotis stoech-*
adifolia grandis). Composite Family
White, three-inch daisy flowers with
pearly petals, undersides lilac-blue.
Gold-rimmed steel-blue centers.

Woolly gray leaves. Makes fine decorative bouquets. Especially floriferous in
a hot, dry spot at the seashore. Also
grows well where summers are cool and
nights heavy with dew. Native of
South Africa.

HEIGHT: 12 to 18 inches.
COLOR: White. Modern hybrid
forms in red, yellow, orange, and in
zones of two or three colors.
LOCATION: Full sun.
SOIL: Light sandy loam.
PLANTING: When nights are
warm, sow seeds where they are to
grow in the open ground. Thin seedlings to stand six to ten inches apart.
USES: Cut-flower arrangements.
Enhances the front of flower borders.
CULTURAL HINTS: Water freely
during the blooming season. To cause
plants to bush out in early summer,
prune back growing points.

BABY BLUE-EYES (*Nemophila menziesii*). Waterleaf Family
From amidst pale green, deeply cut hairy leaves emerge exquisite shallow-cupped flowers, each with an innocent wide-eyed look. The blossoms are about one and one-half inches across. Flourishes where summers, especially nights, are cool and days are misty and often gray. A long drought or hot dry spell discourages the blossoms. If you do not disturb the ground at the end of the season the plants will self-sow and spring up in abundance the following year.
HEIGHT: 6 to 8 inches.
COLOR: Blue, white.
LOCATION: Semishade—sun half the day only.
SOIL: Thrives in any moist soil, but prefers light sandy earth with some humus.
PLANTING: Sow the seeds in March in open ground where they are to grow. In frost-free areas seeds may be sown in September for very early bloom the following spring.
USES: For edging borders and for a damp place in the rock garden.
CULTURAL HINTS: Give ample water during the growing season. Stake gently and carefully, as the flowers suffer from rain damage. The stems and foliage are delicate. Not long-lasting as a cut flower.

◄BABY'S BREATH, ANNUAL (*Gypsophila elegans*). Pink Family
A cloud of white mist in the garden border, a puff of snowy foam in bouquets. This tiny starlike flower is beautiful to grow and a joy to arrange. The blooming period is short and sweet, but the plant is well worth having, nevertheless. Native to Asia Minor and the Caucasus. Grown today in abundance in Europe, Asia and North Africa.
HEIGHT: 12 to 18 inches.
COLOR: White, rose.
LOCATION: Full sun, open position.
SOIL: Light and sandy, not too rich. The Latin name means "chalk-lover."
PLANTING: Sow seeds in the spring in open ground. Space eight inches apart. Will bloom eight weeks from seed. For continuous flowering, sow in succession every two weeks.
USES: For a delicate, misty effect in the flower bed. Lovely cascading over low walls or in hanging baskets.
FRAGRANT. The scent of sweet hay.
CULTURAL HINTS: Give an application of lime when young plants are growing. Wood ashes from the fireplace will be helpful.

BROWALLIA, AMETHYST (*B. americana*). Nightshade Family
Andean Forget-Me-Not from tropical America. Charming five-petaled small blue flowers with a velvety texture all but hide slightly hairy, pointed oval leaves. Blooms all summer and into the fall. A month before the first frost, bring a few plants indoors, trim them way back, and they will bloom all winter, enhancing the sunny window garden.
HEIGHT: 12 to 20 inches.
COLOR: Blue, violet, white.
LOCATION: Full sun or part shade.
SOIL: Grows in average soil but does best if the earth is rich.
PLANTING: Sow seed in the open

ground in May. Thin to eight inches apart. For earlier flowering, buy and set out young plants.

USES: Window boxes, hanging baskets, flower borders, indoor gardens. Fine as cut flowers in arrangements.

CULTURAL HINTS: Pinch out growing points frequently to keep plants compact.

CANDYTUFT, ROCKET (*Iberis amara*). Mustard Family
Named for Iberia, old-time word for Spain, where some species grow magnificently. Flower heads shaped like miniature hyacinths. Bloom a short time, but are well worth growing. Blossoms are the purest white. Unlike most of the flowers in the Mustard Family, whose four petals form a perfect cross (the botanical name for the family is *Cruciferae*), each little flower has two short petals and two long ones. Excellent plants for city gardens, as they can withstand smoke and soot.

HEIGHT: 1 to 2 feet.
COLOR: White.
LOCATION: Full sun. Half sun if you live in a hot dry area.
SOIL: Average, light and well-drained.

PLANTING: In frost-free areas sow seeds in the fall in open ground where they are to grow for June flowers. May be sown in spring also. Thin to six inches apart.

USES: Dramatic border plant. Lovely in indoor bouquets, lasting many days.

FRAGRANT. Fresh, cool sweet scent.

CULTURAL HINTS: To extend the flowering season, sow at two-week intervals. Cut off faded flowers.

CAPE-MARIGOLD, STAR OF THE VELDT (*Dimorphotheca aurantiaca*). Composite Family
This handsome South African Daisy thrives in a dry spot, but does best in summers not too hot. Blossoms close on dark days. Each flower is three and one-half inches across, and the reverse sides of the petals are in shades of blue or lavender. Long blooming season, lasting right up to frost.

HEIGHT: 12 to 18 inches.
COLOR: Rays are orange, lemon, salmon, white; the disk is often violet.
LOCATION: Full sun. Flowers do not open in shade.
SOIL: Light and well-drained; not too rich.
PLANTING: Can be sown indoors in March, and should be in far north states; elsewhere out-of-doors in late spring. Flowers in seven to eight weeks from seed. Thin to ten inches apart. In frost-free areas sow in the fall.

USES: Provides masses of dazzling color throughout the summer in the flower border.

CULTURAL HINTS: To get an early start in flowering, seeds may be sown indoors or in the greenhouse in March.

CALIFORNIA POPPY (*Eschscholtzia californica*). Poppy Family
State flower of California. Appealing blossom buds shaped like peaked green nightcaps. Dazzling orange cup-shaped flowers with slightly frilled edges unfold on sunny days, tossing off these "nightcaps." Delicate silvery-green, finely dissected foliage. Note charming seedpods encircled by a deep pink ruff.
HEIGHT: 1 foot.
COLOR: White, orange, lemon, carmine, pink.
LOCATION: Full sun. A hot and dry spot best.
SOIL: Light and sandy, well-drained, not rich.
PLANTING: Sow in the open ground where plants are to grow; they do not transplant easily.
USES: Fine for covering sunny banks. Thrive in window boxes and planters.
CULTURAL HINTS: In the fall do not disturb the ground where they grew, as these plants often self-sow and come up the following season. Water seedlings freely in the spring.

yellow, dark red, scarlet, pink and green. Blossoms are deep lavender and white, each flower very small, many in a spike; they are not very interesting except under a magnifying glass.
LOCATION: Full or half sun.
SOIL.: Average.
PLANTING: Easiest, and for quick and showy color, is to take tip cuttings of stem or branches at any season and root them in water or damp sand. Then the new plants will be replicas of the old. Seeds are very small and can be sown on damp earth without being covered, and germinate rapidly in warm weather (60 to 70 degrees F). Note that plants grown from seed will not resemble the parent exactly and may, in fact, be entirely different. Set out young plants eight to ten inches apart and keep them shaded from direct sun.
USES: Flower beds, borders, window boxes. May be potted in the fall for your indoor window garden.
CULTURAL HINTS: Pinch off young flower spires and excessive tiny shoots to keep the plant sturdy and large-leaved.

COLEUS (*C. blumei*). Mint Family
From the South Pacific and Southeast Asia. *Koleos* is Greek for "sheath," alluding to the boatlike lower lip that holds and conceals the stamens. Brilliant variegated foliage brings color all summer to the place where this plant grows. Some of the leaves are truly bizarre in their combinations of shades and patterns.
HEIGHT: 6 inches to 2½ feet.
COLOR: Foliage is chartreuse,

CUPFLOWER (*Nierembergia caerulea*). Nightshade Family
Grows wild in the Argentine. Each flower is a lavender cup with a bright yellow eye. Blooms continuously from summer until frost. Mounds of blossoms all but conceal the greenery. Try some of the flower sprays in miniature bouquets, where they have great appeal.
HEIGHT: 6 to 12 inches.
COLOR: Pale or dark lavender or

lavender-blue. Variety 'Purple Robe' is royal violet-purple.

LOCATION: Full sun, or at least morning sun. Some light shade if summers are hot and dry. Shelter from strong winds.

SOIL: Rich loam.

PLANTING: For early bloom, set out young plants eight to ten inches apart. Sow seeds ahead of time indoors or else buy seedlings.

USES: Fine border plant; sturdy, wiry stems make these excellent for edging, window boxes, rock garden.

CULTURAL HINTS: Water often during dry spells. Cut back after flowering. Increase by stem cuttings rooted in sand in late June.

FALSE CHAMOMILE, FEVERFEW (*Matricaria aurea*). Composite Family

From Spain and North Africa. Old-fashioned daisylike flowers with finely divided feathery foliage bloom all summer. Beautiful in the garden and excellent in indoor bouquets. As the name suggests, this plant has medicinal properties, and was said in days gone by to keep away witches. It is also known as Matricary; there is another Feverfew (*Chrysanthemum parthenium*), which has broader, lobed leaves, and similar small daisylike flowers, single and double, but somewhat taller, and quite popular today.

HEIGHT: 6 to 9 inches.

COLOR: Small gold-yellow and white flowers. Also a double form with globular flower heads of soft gold.

LOCATION: Semishade.

SOIL: Average, light, moist loam.

PLANTING: Scatter seeds in the open ground. Thin to stand six inches apart. For earlier bloom sow seeds indoors in late winter.

USES: Plant in dense drifts in the front of the border. For edging paths.

CULTURAL HINTS: Water during dry spells. Mulch lightly to keep the earth slightly damp.

FLOSSFLOWER (*Ageratum houstonianum*). Composite Family

Our Ageratum of today is descended from a Mexican wild plant. The misty blue heads of flowers are soft and furry to touch. Lovely mingled in the flower border with sweet alyssum, love-in-a-mist, purple or white petunias, and many lemon-yellow flowers. The showy blooms last a long time, and keep coming from June to September.

HEIGHT: 3 to 6 inches, usually.

COLOR: Usually lavender or blue-violet, but also white, pink and darker blue varieties.

LOCATION: Full sun or light shade.

SOIL: Average.

PLANTING: Sow seed indoors in mid-March or April, depending on your latitude. Seeds germinate in about a week but grow slowly. Or buy young plants from a local dealer. Set out plants five to six inches apart.

USES: Window boxes, flower borders, edgings of paths. Makes attractive small bouquets. Lovely as a pot plant in the indoor garden.

CULTURAL HINTS: For continuous bloom snip off fading flowers. If white fly attacks the plants, spray with Malathion.

▲

KINGFISHER DAISY (*Felicia bergeriana*). Composite Family
A sky-blue Daisy with gold center, from South Africa. Especially good in Southern gardens, where it becomes a dainty and fine edging plant. Each bloom, three-quarters of an inch across, is solitary on its stalk, rising from a dense carpet of oval gray-green leaves. True sun-lovers, they fold up on cloudy days. In the South, they often winter over.

HEIGHT: 6 inches.

COLOR: Sky-blue, sometimes white.

LOCATION: Full sun.

SOIL: Thrives in a rather light soil made up of sandy loam and leaf mold.

PLANTING: Seeds can be sown in the open ground. For a longer blooming period plant indoors at the end of winter. Set out in a sheltered, sunny spot eight inches apart.

USES: Dry pockets in rock gardens. To border walks and beds. Good for balcony planters and window boxes, as they are impervious to wind.

CULTURAL HINTS: Feed during the summer for a profusion of flowers.

LOBELIA (*L. erinus speciosa*). Lobelia Family
From the Cape of Good Hope comes this vivid flower of the same electric blue as the sea in October. Foliage is an attractive dark metallic green, toothed along the margins. The blooms, growing in profusion, are white-throated. In the African Mountains of the Moon (Ruwenzori Range), other species of Lobelia attain a height of thirty feet; the flower spike, resembling an obelisk, is pollinated by sunbirds.

HEIGHT: 6 to 10 inches. There are dwarf erect varieties and partly trailing forms.

COLOR: Blue. Also other varieties in lavender, deep blue, carmine, pink, white.

LOCATION: Full sun. In hot dry areas, give partial shade.

SOIL: Rich, loose, friable earth.

PLANTING: Set out young plants six inches apart. Buy seedlings or sow seed indoors not later than mid-March. Seed is very small and slow to germinate.

USES: A fine border plant. Good in hanging baskets and window boxes. Especially charming combined with bright red geraniums. Excellent in

▼

rock gardens and as a ground cover.

CULTURAL HINTS: Must be kept watered during dry spells. Shear in midsummer to promote later bloom.

MEXICAN DWARF MARIGOLD
(*Tagetes tenuifolia pumila*). Composite Family

Small, striped flowers emerge from deeply cut foliage. One of the easiest and best-loved of all flowers to grow. In Mexico, where these flourish wild, they are often fed to the hens, and the subsequent eggs delight the Mexican housewife with their dark orange yolks. These plants have great value to gardeners as, wherever they grow, they free the soil from nematodes, and are frequently planted between rows of vegetables by organic gardeners.

HEIGHT: 6 to 10 inches.

COLOR: Gold, lemon, orange, maroon-marked.

▼

LOCATION: Thrives in a hot, sunny, dry spot, an open area free from encroaching bushes and trees.

SOIL: Light, well-drained, moderately rich earth.

PLANTING: Sow seeds in the spring where they are to grow. Thin seedlings to six inches apart. For earlier blooms, buy plants from a nursery.

USES: Borders, edgings, window boxes, planters, terrace pots. A good and lasting cut flower.

FRAGRANT. Pungent foliage and flowers. Many, if not most, people dislike the smell.

CULTURAL HINTS: For continuous bloom trim off faded flowers.

MEADOW-FOAM (*Limnanthes douglasii*). Limnanthes Family

Native to our West Coast mountains. The trailing, deeply cut leaves are an interesting yellowish green. The one-inch five-petaled fragrant blossoms are like gold, pink or white stars. The greenery forms a dense carpet that in summer is smothered with an abundance of blossoms. Among the most free-flowering of all annuals. Also called Poached-Egg Flower.

HEIGHT: 12 inches.

COLOR: Yellow, white-tipped or rose-tinged.

LOCATION: Open, sunny position.

SOIL: Regular garden loam.

PLANTING: Sow seeds in the open ground where it is to flower. Successive sowings desirable, as the plants go to seed in a few weeks. May be planted in autumn in frost-free areas. Thin seedlings to four inches apart. Needs cool nights in summer.

USES: Edging for garden paths. Grow in drifts in the border. Will carpet the earth anywhere. Attractive pot plant. Beloved by bees.

FRAGRANT. Delicate fresh scent.

CULTURAL HINTS: Roots must be kept cool and moist. If you don't disturb the ground in the fall, the self-sown seeds will come up next spring.

MIGNONETTE (*Reseda odorata*). ▶
Mignonette Family
A native of North Africa, Arabia and
Persia. Here is a plant grown mainly
for the sweet scent that drifts far and
wide. One small patch will perfume
the whole garden. Napoleon collected
some of this seed in Egypt and sent it
to Josephine. Does best in a cool
area, where its blooming season will be
from June to October—the season is
much shorter in a hot, dry climate.

HEIGHT: 1 to 1½ feet.
COLOR: Green-yellow, brown-red,
yellow-white.
LOCATION: Part shade.
SOIL: Fertile soil, with some lime.
PLANTING: Sow thinly where it is
to flower, press lightly with a board,
but do not cover. Do not, if possible,
transplant at all; just thin to stand
six inches apart.
USES: Plant by the front door or
under a window where the scent
floats in. In pots on the windowsill.
Add to indoor arrangements.
FRAGRANT. A penetrating scent.
The lower-growing and less showy
kinds are apt to be more fragrant than
the "improved" modern cultivars.
CULTURAL HINTS: For bushy
plants, pinch growing tips when seedlings are four inches high. Do not
disturb roots when cultivating the bed.

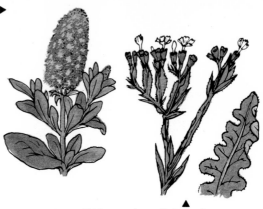

SOIL: Light, sandy, well-drained
loam.
PLANTING: Sow in the open
ground in spring, thin to stand one foot
apart. Or sow indoors about mid-
March. The seeds are held in the dried
flowers and are sometimes sold this
way—in which case pick the clusters
apart and plant pieces on their sides.
USES: Fine for cut flowers in
summer and excellent in dried winter
bouquets.
CULTURAL HINTS: For dried-
flower arrangements, cut the flowers
when they are wide open, hang upside
down in bunches in a shady place until
they are completely dry.

STATICE, SEA LAVENDER
(*Limonium sinuatum*). Plumbago
Family
Native to Mediterranean regions.
Scalloped leaves lie flat on the soil.
Emerging from these are rough,
branching flower stems with small
tissue-paperlike blossoms, which dry
readily and last in bouquets all winter.
Limonium, from the Greek *leimon*,
means "meadow"; and the genus does
thrive in salt meadows watered by high
tides and inlets.
HEIGHT: 1 foot.
COLOR: Lavender, pink, yellow,
white.
LOCATION: Full sun. Especially
good in seaside gardens.

PETUNIA (*P. hybrida*). Nightshade
Family
First discovered in Brazil. Here is a
plant that adapts to just about every
kind of climate and condition. Comes
in a large assortment of colors, and
the blossoms vary in character. They
are double or single, large or small,
streaked, starred, striped, fringed,
ruffled, plain. Certain varieties may be
four inches across, others one inch.
Flowers freely in hot, dry summers.
HEIGHT: 6 to 15 inches.
COLOR: Shades of crimson, scarlet, magenta, pink, blue, pale yellow,
and white.
LOCATION: A warm, sunny place.
Will tolerate partial shade.

▲

Soil: Adapts well to all kinds of earth, but prefers loamy, fertile soil that is slightly acid.

Planting: Sow seed in the open ground. Separate to stand eight inches apart. To hasten early bloom, buy plants in bud in the spring.

Uses: Garden borders and beds. Trailing from window boxes, planters and hanging baskets. Fine for cut flowers.

Fragrant. Subtly scented by day; very sweet at night.

Cultural hints: For compact growth and ample bloom trim plants back a few times during the summer. Feed often and water abundantly. For control of white fly spray with Malathion.

PHACELIA (*P. campanularia*). Water-leaf Family
Wide, bell-shaped pure blue blooms with prominent white-tipped stamens are produced in profusion all summer. They face upward from small mounds of scalloped leaves and interesting reddish stems. Phacelia does best in a climate where nights are cool.

Height: 6 to 9 inches.

Color: An intense gentian blue.

Location: Full sun, where it is hot and dry.

Soil: Light and sandy.

Planting: Sow seed in the open ground where plants are to grow. When two inches high, thin to stand eight inches apart. Difficult to transplant except when very small.

Uses: Creates delightful low

borders. Effective when grown in masses. Good in rock gardens.

Fragrant. When leaves are bruised they have a pleasant odor.

Cultural hints: Pinch back young seedlings to strengthen the plant and for more blooms.

▲

PHLOX, ANNUAL; TEXAS PRIDE (*P. drummondii*). Phlox Family
An enchanting and foolproof flower for beginners. By midsummer each plant becomes a solid mound of blossoms. A sweep of these blooms is a small garden in itself because of the great variety of shades and colors. Especially sweet-scented at dusk and in the evening. From Texas grasslands and coastal plains.

Height: 8 to 18 inches.

Color: White, buff, shades of pink, rose, lavender, all with contrasting eye.

Location: Full sun.

Soil: Sandy, slightly enriched, slightly acid, well drained.

Planting: Sow in the open ground where plants are to grow; or indoors in March—but seedlings do not always transplant readily.

Uses: Excellent in rock gardens, window boxes. Make delightful bouquets.

Fragrant. The scent of meadow grass in the sun.

Cultural hints: Trim off faded flowers to extend the blooming period. When plants straggle, trim back to four to six inches and soon they send up new buds.

▲
PIMPERNEL (*Anagallis arvensis*).
Primrose Family
This is the native Scarlet Pimpernel
of Europe, naturalized to some extent
in eastern United States. It is often
called Shepherd's Clock or Poor Man's
Weather Glass because it opens in
sunshine and closes when rain is coming. A trailing plant that must be kept
under control. The plain but endearing little flowers are on branching
axillary stems. Blooms from July to
October.

HEIGHT: 6 inches.
COLOR: Scarlet, salmon, white.
LOCATION: A hot, dry, sunny
place.
SOIL: Light and sandy.
PLANTING: Sow in the open
ground where it is to grow, in April-
May. Space six inches apart.
USES: For nooks in the rock
garden. For the tops of sunny walls,
or cracks and crevices. Hanging baskets.
CULTURAL HINTS: For a longer
period of bloom, start the seeds indoors
in March.

◀ PINK, CHINA (*Dianthus chinensis
heddewigii*). Pink Family
Native to East Asia. Five-petaled
flowers with fringed edges (and also
"double" flowers with many petals)
emerge from attractive slender gray-
green foliage. For larger flowers,
remove all but the top bud on each
stem. This species will self-sow if the
earth around is undisturbed in summer
and early fall.

HEIGHT: 6 to 12 inches.
COLOR: Crimson, red, maroon,
salmon, lilac.
LOCATION: Full sun.
SOIL: Well-drained alkaline soil.
PLANTING: Sow in the open
ground where plants are to grow; thin
to six inches apart. For earlier blooms,
sow indoors in March, and keep the
young plants in comparatively cool
temperature.
USES: For garden edgings. Very
effective when grown in masses. A bouquet will scent the whole room.
FRAGRANT. Spicy, lingering scent.
CULTURAL HINTS: Cover with
straw in late fall, and they will live
over winter if the weather is not too
severe. Lightly add lime or wood
ashes during the summer to keep the
soil alkaline.

▲
PORTULACA, ROSE MOSS
(*P. grandiflora*). Purslane Family
An annual from Brazil. The dazzling

flower, single or double, is like a miniature rose. Opens each sunny morning to form a carpet of color. Reddish stems and fleshy leaves are all but obscured by the carpet of blooms.

HEIGHT: 4 to 6 inches.

COLOR: Pink, apricot, flame, yellow, red, white.

LOCATION: Full sun, the hottest place in your garden.

SOIL: Light, dry, sandy and poor. Adapts to other soils, except clay.

PLANTING: In late April or early May, sow seeds in rows made by pressing a narrow board or lath just into the soil where they are to grow. Thin out seedlings to about six inches apart.

USES: Covers a sunny bank, the edge of a driveway, patio planters.

CULTURAL HINTS: Will endure neglect and drought.

SWAN RIVER DAISY (*Brachycome iberidifolia*). Composite Family

Try this seldom seen delicately foliaged plant from Western Australia and enjoy its unusual half-inch starry flowers and compact habit. Each blossom has a disc in the center. The center is strongly convex, with dark, tubular disk florets.

HEIGHT: 18 inches.

COLOR: Blue, purple, pink, white.

▼

LOCATION: Full sun. Shelter from wind.

SOIL: Rich earth.

PLANTING: Set out young plants from seed sown indoors in March or purchased plants. Space six inches apart.

USES: Borders, window boxes, terrace planters; good as a cut flower.

CULTURAL HINTS: Place small branches between the seedlings so that the slender stems, as they grow, will receive support and remain upright.

TOADFLAX (*Linaria bipartita*). Snapdragon Family

A miniature member of a rather large family, native to Portugal and North Africa. Delightful in groups in the front of the bed, where each plant becomes a mound of gay flowers.

HEIGHT: 9 to 12 inches.

COLOR: Yellow, purple, crimson, white, pink, lavender.

LOCATION: Open sunny position.

SOIL: Light and sandy and well-drained. Will adapt to other soils.

PLANTING: Sow seed in the open ground where the plant is to grow. Thin to six inches apart.

USES: Rock gardens, edgings, miniature arrangements.

CULTURAL HINTS: Don't try to transplant; merely thin.

▼

VERBENA *(V. hortensis)*. Verbena Family
Colorful flower heads composed of countless small florets stand just above abundant, toothed, soft green leaves. They provide spreading patches in the front of the perennial border and can stretch out irregularly across the lawn or path. One species of Verbena was among the sacred herbs used in Roman times to sweep the altar of Jupiter. Our garden plants are hybrids of South American varieties.

HEIGHT: Trails along the ground, rooting as it goes. Some varieties 1 foot tall.

COLOR: White, pink, red, lavender, purple. Many varieties have white eyes.

LOCATION: Full sun.

SOIL: Average.

PLANTING: Seed may be sown out-of-doors in May for late-summer bloom. For earlier bloom, sow seed indoors in March and set out six inches apart in May. Plants just beginning to bloom may be bought in nurseries in the spring, and you can select the colors you want. Plants from seed may not all come true to the specified colors.

USES: A good, if rather high, ground cover. Fine for beds and edgings. Does well in rock gardens.

CULTURAL HINTS: If covered with dry leaves and branches, Verbena may winter over if climate is not too severe. Or it may be potted up and brought indoors for cuttings to be taken in spring.

▼

▲

WISHBONE FLOWER *(Torenia fournieri)*. Snapdragon Family
A plant from the tropics of Asia and Africa. In the throat of the trumpet-shaped blossom you will see a pair of stamens formed into a tiny white wishbone. If there has been a cool, wet summer, the foliage turns an interesting reddish hue.

HEIGHT: 10 inches.

COLOR: Violet and lavender, yellow blotch on lower lip.

LOCATION: Partial shade and sheltered from wind.

SOIL: Light and sandy, warm and moist.

PLANTING: Sow seeds indoors in March and set out young plants in May. When seedlings are two inches high, set them nine inches apart. Or buy young plants at a nursery.

USES: Garden borders, pots and low-hanging baskets, perhaps combined with a few pendent vines, edging patios and walks. A different house plant, amusing and endearing—the flowers are like odd little faces.

CULTURAL HINTS: Grows best where the earth is slightly moist and where nights are cool. Water freely in warm weather.

CREEPING ZINNIA *(Sanvitalia* ▶ *procumbens)*. Composite Family
Here is a rare and exciting little Zinnia relative, like a miniature sunflower, with a dark center and light yellow rays. There are also double and semi-

double varieties. Blooms from June to frost, and deserves to be better known. It trails along the ground, sending up vertical or curving branches producing one-inch-wide flower heads. Grows wild on the mesas of Mexico.

HEIGHT: 6 inches.

COLOR: Yellow, purple-centered.

LOCATION: Full sun.

SOIL: Light and well-drained.

PLANTING: Sow indoors in March and transplant carefully to outdoors six inches apart.

USES: Will trail down over a wall, bank or slope. Give a dry position in the rock garden.

CULTURAL HINTS: If winters are mild, sow outdoors in September for a long-summer flowering the following year.

ZINNIA, LILLIPUT (Z. *angustifolia*). Composite Family

Here is a delightful miniature double flower that blooms freely from July to frost. Blossoms are one-and-one-half inches across. Zinnias are natives of South America and Mexico, and in the sixteenth century were among the favorite flowers in the gardens of Montezuma. Named in honor of J. G. Zinn, a professor of botany at Gottingen University. This very small variety is a horticultural form. (See also below and pages 30, 63, 64.)

HEIGHT: 6 to 10 inches.

COLOR: Tawny reds, crimson, scarlet, yellow, orange, pink, and also white; usually darker centered.

LOCATION: Full sun.

SOIL: Light and sandy, moderately enriched.

PLANTING: Sow in the open ground in spring. Thin to stand six inches apart.

USES: Borders, edging walks and drives. Makes stunning bouquets.

CULTURAL HINTS: Keep withered flower heads picked off for continuous bloom.

ZINNIA 'PERSIAN CARPET'

(variety of Z. *angustifolia*). Composite Family

Petals interestingly two-toned and tipped with contrasting color. Years ago, zinnias were frequently called "Youth and Old Age" because while the ray flowers are aging, new disk flowers are appearing in the center of the bloom. The 'Persian Carpet' strain is a fairly recent cultivar of the species *angustifolia* and retains the same type of long narrow leaves. Quantities of this strain in mixed colors are indeed evocative of an Oriental rug.

HEIGHT: 6 to 8 inches.

COLOR: Every shade but blue.

LOCATION: Full sun.

SOIL: Light, sandy loam, moderately rich.

PLANTING: Sow in the open ground in May; thin to stand eight inches apart.

USES: Borders, massed color in the flower bed, hot, dry spots in the rock garden, indoor bouquets.

CULTURAL HINTS: Keep withered flower heads picked off for continuous bloom.

MEDIUM

▲

BALSAM; LADY-SLIPPER
(*Impatiens balsamina*). Balsam Family
From India, Malay and China comes
this unusual plant with lovely
camellia-like flowers growing up and
down the stalk. An old-time favorite
garden plant, introduced into Europe
in the sixteenth century. Listen to
the popping noise as the curiously
shaped fruits shake out their seeds
in late summer and fall.

HEIGHT: 15 to 24 inches.
COLOR: White, flesh, salmon,
rose, purple, violet.
LOCATION: Full sun or partial
shade.
SOIL: Light, sandy loam, somewhat rich and moist.
PLANTING: Sow seed in the open
ground in May. Thin to stand ten
inches apart.
USES: Delightful and unusual
addition to the flower border.
CULTURAL HINTS: May be trans-
planted in full bloom to rearrange the
border if desired. When grown in
an exposed position, stake. Soak the
seeds twenty-four hours before sowing.
Responds well to extra feeding in
summer.

BELLS-OF-IRELAND (*Molucella
laevis*). Mint Family
White-veined green "flowers" cling up
and down an upright stalk with a
tuft of leaves on top. The stems and
flowers dry successfully for indoor
winter decoration. Originally from the
eastern Mediterranean region, where it
grows wild. Actually, the little flower
is in the center of the green enclosing
calyx; the calyx is not really bell-
shaped; and the original plant is a
native of Israel and Asia Minor, so the
common name is hardly justified.

HEIGHT: 20 inches.
COLOR: Green.
LOCATION: Full sun.
SOIL: Average garden loam.
PLANTING: Sow seeds in the open
ground in early spring where they are
to grow. Don't transplant, but thin
to nine inches apart.
USES: Good cut flowers. Fine in
dried arrangements.
FRAGRANT.
CULTURAL HINTS: Dry in a cool,
dark, airy spot. Trim the leaves off
first to best display the bells.

▼

BLUE LACEFLOWER (*Trachymene caerulea*). Carrot Family
From Australia comes this plant with furry stems and leaves topped by a three-inch-wide parasol of delicate tiny blue florets. Each one is exquisite when magnified. The blossom is like a glamorized, pale blue version of wild carrot, or Queen Anne's Lace.

HEIGHT: 18 inches.
COLOR: Powder blue.
LOCATION: Full sun, sheltered position.
SOIL: Light garden loam, moderately rich.
PLANTING: Sow in the open ground where they are to grow, and separate to stand nine inches apart. For earlier bloom, sow seed indoors in March.
USES: Fine in bouquets, lasting many days, and especially effective with yellow snapdragons as complementary color and form.
FRAGRANT. The fragrance of tall ▶ grass in the sun.
CULTURAL HINTS: Does best where nights are cool and well below 70 degrees F. It languishes in hot weather. Support with brushwood to hold upright on windy days and in rainstorms.

BLUE THIMBLE FLOWER (*Gilia capitata*). Phlox Family
Here is a plant native to the western part of our own country, with interesting globular or dome-shaped heads of light blue flowers. The leaves are intricately divided, dainty and feathery; some are ribbonlike and often forked at the tips.

HEIGHT: 2 feet.
COLOR: Light blue to lavender.
LOCATION: Open, sunny position.
SOIL: Moderately rich.
PLANTING: Sow in the open ground where they are to grow. Do not transplant, but thin to stand six inches apart.
USES: Excellent for cutting. Charming in the flower border.

CULTURAL HINTS: Stake the plants to prevent their blowing over in storms. ▼

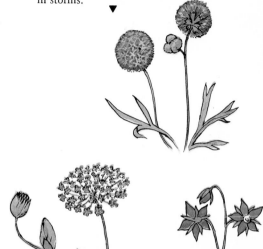

BORAGE (*Borago officinalis*). ▲
Borage Family
Silver downy stems and buds, starry blue flowers with deep purple anthers. Borage, they say, brings "alwaies courage." Toss a few of the flowers into the salad, and who knows? Also said to "exhilarate and make the minde glad." A mecca for bees in the area, which hum and buzz among the flowers all day long.

HEIGHT: 15 to 30 inches.
COLOR: Pure sky blue.
LOCATION: Full sun.
SOIL: Light and sandy.
PLANTING: Sow in the open ground and thin to stand ten inches apart.
USES: The blue flowers are delicious in salads. Lovely in arrangements indoors.
CULTURAL HINTS: Best not to transplant, but to thin and leave the plants where you want them.

CALANDRINIA (*C. ciliata*).
Purslane Family ▶
From Peru and Ecuador. A cousin to
the familiar portulaca, with rather
similar short-lived blooms, fleshy, but
wider and longer leaves, and a more
erect habit, but a delight in its own
right. Flowers open only in the
sunshine and close on cloudy days.
HEIGHT: 12 inches.
COLOR: Purple, red, rose, white.
LOCATION: Open area and
full sun.
SOIL: Average, and not too rich.
PLANTING: Sow thickly in open
ground. Thin to stand four inches
apart.
USES: Excellent for edgings, rock
gardens and window boxes.
CULTURAL HINTS: Do not disturb
the ground around the plants in late
summer and fall; the self-sown seeds
will come up the following spring.

CIGAR-FLOWER (*Cuphea
platycentra*). Loosestrife Family
Unusual tubular flowers, consisting of
a bright red calyx with a black-and-
white tip, suggesting a cigar ash.
The flowers swing among lance-shaped
leaves and make a vivid display in
the border. A native of Mexico, where
it is a perennial.
HEIGHT: To 1 foot or more.
COLOR: Scarlet.
LOCATION: Full sun, light shade.
SOIL: Average.
PLANTING: Best results come
from setting out young plants (nine
inches apart). Sow seed indoors right
after Christmas, or buy plants in
the spring.
USES: An everblooming plant for
the window garden. For window boxes,
hanging baskets and rock garden.
CULTURAL HINTS: It takes these
lovely flowers four or five months
from seed to bloom, so you must give
them a good head start indoors. To be
sure of bushy, compact growth, pinch
◀ out tips of young plants.

CLARKIA (*C. elegans*). Evening-
Primrose Family
A popular native of our Western states,
particularly California. Named for
Captain William Clark, of the Lewis
and Clark expedition. Does not do
well in a hot climate. If you live where
nights are chilly, the spikes of showy
flowers on reddish stems make a fine
garden display and are excellent for

▲

cutting. Blooms from July to October.
The flower's shape resembles the
Maltese cross.

HEIGHT: To 2 feet.

COLOR: Rosy-purple, lilac, white.
There are even more showy modern
double-flowering cultivars in delicate
pink, salmon, scarlet.

LOCATION: Half sun, full sun.

SOIL: Easily grown in warm, light
soil containing humus. Responds to a
dressing of well-rotted manure.

PLANTING: Set out young plants
nine inches apart or sow outdoors
as early as possible in the spring. Seeds
may be sown in the fall if your climate
is mild.

USES: A good bedding plant.

FRAGRANT. A deep, penetrating
scent.

CULTURAL HINTS: Feed frequently
with superphosphate or any good
garden fertilizer.

CORNFLOWER; BACHELOR'S ▶
BUTTON; RAGGED SAILOR
(*Centaurea cyanus*). Composite
Family
The goldfinches hover over the plants
for the tweedy seeds that develop
during the summer. Dried flowers
found in the tomb of Tutankhamen
were still deep blue. The foliage is
light green or gray-green. The combination is enchanting. Long ago, it is
said, the sky sent down to the corn and
wheat fields small chinks of itself in the

form of these flowers in response to
their desire to commune with the
heavens. Ever after, the Cornflower ran
rampant through the fields of Europe
and Britain, there to be woven into
garlands by children.

HEIGHT: 2½ feet.

COLOR: White, blue, pink,
lavender.

LOCATION: Full sun, sheltered
position.

SOIL: Average, light, well-drained
soil. Avoid overrich earth.

PLANTING: Sow in the open
ground early in the spring and thin the
seedlings to stand six inches apart.

USES: Fine border plant. Excellent for pot culture and good in the
greenhouse.

CULTURAL HINTS: Save a few seed
heads for the birds, but keep the rest
picked off for continuous bloom.

▲
DAHLIA (*D. coccinea* and hybrids).
Composite Family
Dahlia, which flourished in the gardens
of the Aztecs, is now the official flower
(all species) of Mexico. It comes in
wonderful, rich tapestry colors. It is
named in honor of Andreas Dahl, a
Swedish botanist. Petals add flavor,
color and interest to salads. Horticul-
turists originally thought this plant
would be a rival of the potato, but
alas, the flavor of the tubers was a
disappointment. The Indians, however,
used them as a tonic.

HEIGHT: 2 to 3 feet.

COLOR: All shades of yellow,
orange and red, also white, lavender,
some very dark purples and rich
maroon.

LOCATION: Open, sunny position.

SOIL: Well-drained sandy soil,
not too rich.

PLANTING: Sow seeds indoors in
March. Set out young plants ten inches
to one foot apart.

USES: Small groups in the border
—or in rows, for cutting and for easier
cultivation. Cut flowers are long-lasting.

CULTURAL HINTS: Water freely in
hot, dry weather. Feed generously at
intervals during the summer. Tubers
can be taken up before frost, cleaned
and stored in sand or polyethylene bags
in a cool place over winter. They should
be checked at intervals and not allowed
to dry out or to get too damp. In the
spring they can be divided, with each
tuber of the clump keeping one bud or
eye. Use a sharp knife for this.

FORGET-ME-NOT, CHINESE ▲
(*Cynoglossum amabile*). Borage
Family
A short period of bloom, but worth-
while for its interesting coarse, hairy
foliage and long sprays of deep vibrant
blue flowers. Forms compact bushy
clumps. As blue as the sea in October
or a mountain lake in the fall. An ancient myth tells of a cup of nectar
made from the sky and being given to
one of the goddesses by her lover. As
he passed it to her, it spilled on the
ground, and up sprang the Forget-Me-
Not.

HEIGHT: 1½ to 2 feet.

COLOR: Blue.

LOCATION: Hot, dry, sunny position. Will also do fairly well in partial
shade.

SOIL: Light and sandy.

PLANTING. Set out young plants
twelve inches apart. Give them a head
start by sowing seed in the house in
March.

USES: A fine note of blue in the
border. Attractive and long-lasting as a
cut flower.

CULTURAL HINTS: Will scatter
their seeds and come up again the
following year if the earth where they
grow is not disturbed. The plant is
really a biennial where conditions are
right for it.

GAILLARDIA, PAINTED (G.   ▶
pulchella hybrids). Composite Family
Gaillardia has sunset colors, a long

season of bloom, and it likes heat and drought. Named after M. Gaillard de Marentonneau, a French patron of botany. Flourishes in abundance in the pastures of Nebraska, where it is as colorful as an Oriental rug.

HEIGHT: 18 inches to 2 feet.

COLOR: The original species has single daisylike flowers with yellow rays, red-purple at the base, but now there are also shaggy double varieties and semidoubles in many shades of red, orange, yellow, maroon and white.

LOCATION: Full sun, warm sheltered position. Withstands heat and drought.

SOIL: Light, sandy and rich; succumbs in heavy soil.

PLANTING: Sow seeds in the open ground. Space seedlings to stand eight inches apart.

USES: Fine for window boxes and planters, as plants tolerate dry soil. Excellent cut flowers. Does well in the greenhouse.

CULTURAL HINTS: The taller plants may need staking.

GLOBE AMARANTH (*Gomphrena globosa*). Amaranthus Family
Like large heads of clover. Pick fully developed flowers and hang upside down to dry for winter bouquets. Amaranth means "immortal flower." Found in the tropics the world over, and delighting in hot days and nights. Stands up well in wind and rain. The plant was introduced into Holland from Southeast Asia around 1670 and into England in the early 1700's. It was popular in Colonial gardens in the United States. ▼

HEIGHT: To 18 inches.

COLOR: White, rose, purple, orange, sometimes yellow.

LOCATION: Full sun.

SOIL: Deep, rich, well-drained loam.

PLANTING: Sow seeds outdoors and space eight inches apart. They may take up to two weeks to germinate. For a longer season of bloom, plant indoors at the end of winter; or buy and set out young plants.

USES: Window boxes, planters. Dried flowers in winter arrangements.

CULTURAL HINTS: Give ample water in a dry spell.

GOLDENCUP; MEXICAN TULIP-POPPY (*Hunnemannia fumariaefolia*). Poppy Family
Comes from Mexico. Petals are interestingly creased and crinkled. Each three-inch satiny blossom is a chink of golden sunshine. Blooms from July to September. Glaucous foliage is delicately divided but dense.

HEIGHT: 2 feet.

COLOR: Yellow.

LOCATION: Full sun.

SOIL: Average loam.

PLANTING: Sow in the open ground in the spring where it is to flower. Thin plants to twelve inches apart.

USES: For covering warm, sunny slopes. Lovely in the border. Splendid for cutting. Cut in bud and singe the stems, or dip briefly in boiling water; they will last a week.

CULTURAL HINTS: Leave the ground undisturbed in the fall, and the self-sown seeds will produce new plants next spring. ▼

HELIOTROPE; CHERRY PIE ▶
(*Heliotropium arborescens*). Borage
Family

For a lovely color combination, plant
with pink petunias and white alyssum.
Dry blossoms on the windowsill for a
sachet. A Victorian favorite, it was
brought originally from Ecuador and
Peru, where it grows as a tall shrub or
vine. The name Heliotrope means
"constantly turning to face the sun."

HEIGHT: 1 to 2 feet, sometimes
higher.

COLOR: Violet.

LOCATION: Full sun.

SOIL: Rich, sandy loam.

PLANTING: Set out young plants
one foot apart for all-summer bloom.
Start seeds indoors in midwinter; or
buy young seedlings.

USES: Colorful and fragrant for
the border, window boxes and terrace
pots. Adds character and scent to mixed
bouquets.

FRAGRANT. Rather like vanilla and
narcissus.

CULTURAL HINTS: If plants are
grown in pots, give a bit of shade
during the day.

LANTANA (*L. camara*). Verbena
Family

A perfect plant for bordering drives, for
containers and on terraces. Pot up in
the fall and bring indoors to a sunny
window, where it will thrive for weeks.
First discovered in Jamaica in the late
seventeenth century, it now grows wild
in the southern United States, where it
carpets fields and thrives along roadsides.

HEIGHT: 12 to 18 inches. Some
varieties are gracefully trailing.

COLOR: Blossoms open yellow,
turning to orange and red; frequently
all colors are mingled in the same flat
cluster.

LOCATION: Full sun. Will tolerate
part shade.

SOIL: Rich soil, but fairly
adaptable.

PLANTING: Sow seeds indoors in
February and set out seedlings one foot
apart, or buy plants.

USES: Makes a fine accent plant
on terraces and in gardens. Also good in
hanging baskets and window boxes.
Thrives at the shore.

FRAGRANT. Both flowers and
leaves have a pungent scent.

CULTURAL HINTS: When the
plants straggle, trim them back for a
more compact habit.

FLAX, FLOWERING (*Linum
grandiflorum*). Flax Family

A lovely plant from North Africa. A
source of both linen cloth and linseed-
oil poultices. Each flower lasts but a
day. However, countless more keep
coming and unfolding amidst grasslike
foliage.

HEIGHT: 18 inches to 2 feet.

COLOR: Blue, red, pink, scarlet,
white. The red form is remarkably
brilliant.

LOCATION: Full sun. Sheltered position.

SOIL: Light, sandy, well-drained earth.

PLANTING: Sow outdoors where plants are to grow. Do not try to transplant, but thin to stand eight inches apart.

USES: Colorful border plant. Enhances the spot where it grows. Charming in bouquets.

CULTURAL HINTS: Does best where summers are cool. Sow seeds in succession for continuous bloom; each plant blooms only three or four weeks. Stake to protect from wind damage.

▼

LOVE-IN-A-MIST; FENNEL FLOWER (*Nigella damascena*). Buttercup Family

Originally from Damascus, it grows wild now in Mediterranean countries. Flowers are set in a fringe of feathery foliage and develop into pale green urn-shaped or globular seedpods. In the sixteenth century the plant was cultivated for its aromatic seeds, somewhat like cinnamon, and used as a spice. In Egypt the seeds have been sprinkled on bread and cakes from the time of the Pharaohs to the present day. They were favored by Egyptian ladies to insure the plumpness that

▼

▲

IMMORTELLE (*Xeranthemum annuum*). Composite Family

Native to the Mediterranean region. Dry the papery blossoms for use in winter bouquets. Appealing lance-shaped, woolly white leaves.

HEIGHT: 2 to 3 feet.

COLOR: Lavender, rose, pink, red, white.

LOCATION: Open, sunny position.

SOIL: Rather poor dry soil.

PLANTING: Sow seeds in the open ground. Thin to six inches apart.

USES: In dried bouquets. A colorful touch in the flower border.

CULTURAL HINTS: Stake the plants or insert brushwood for support. Cut when fully opened. Gather in bunches, hang upside down in a cool, airy place to dry.

was considered an attribute of beauty in that part of the world.

HEIGHT: 18 to 24 inches.

COLOR: Blue, white, old rose.

LOCATION: Sun and open, airy position.

SOIL: Light garden loam, well-drained.

PLANTING: Sow seeds in the open ground. Space seedlings eight inches apart. Thin rather than transplant.

USES: Fine for cut flowers. The green seedpods, dried, are excellent in winter arrangements. Sow seed again in late June for September–October flowers.

CULTURAL HINTS: Stake plants. Cut the stalk when the pods are mature and hang heads down in a shady place to dry.

Should have gypsum and wood ashes to give calcium.

PLANTING: Sow where it is to grow. It takes eight weeks from seed to flower. Do not transplant. Thin to stand ten inches apart.

USES: Dramatic in the flower border, they also make exciting cut flowers.

CULTURAL HINTS: These plants thrive best in areas of long, cool springs and summers. Like all members of the Pea Family, Lupines need nitrogen, and they are largely dependent upon a special bacteria that converts nitrogen into a form plants can absorb. Seed can be treated with legume bacteria culture, sold under various names (Nitracin, Legume-Aid, etc.) by some seed stores. Or you may be able to mix a few spadefuls of soil where Lupines are already growing into your fresh soil.

FRENCH MARIGOLD (*Tagetes patula*). Composite Family

Brought to England first by Huguenot refugees, hence the name "French." Actually it grows wild in Mexico, and some early traveler took seeds from there to France. Brilliant gold and/or mahogany flowers produced in profusion are one and one-half inches across. Some are single, some very double. Nice foliage. An amiable plant that blooms from early summer well beyond the first light frost or two, it is a great joy in the late-fall garden. Especially useful because nematodes disappear from the ground where these Marigolds are grown.

HEIGHT: 12 inches or more.

COLOR: Gold or mahogany, some flowers two-toned.

LOCATION: Sun and open position where the ranging plant may have ample space around it.

SOIL: Light, moderately rich, well-drained sandy loam.

PLANTING: Sow seed in the open ground. Transplant to stand six inches apart.

▲

LUPINE (*Lupinus hartwegii*). Pea Family

Deeply slashed leaves are as lovely as the flowers. Great spires of blossoms tower in dignity above the foliage. It was an old-time belief that a diet of Lupine and water stimulated flights of fancy. Protogenes, a famous painter from Rhodes in the third century B.C., is said to have painted masterpieces while on this diet.

HEIGHT: 3 feet.

COLOR: The true species has blue flowers touched with rose, but now there are horticultural varieties in shades of red and pink, also in white.

LOCATION: Half sun and half shade, also full sun.

SOIL: Sandy loam, neutral and not too rich. Does well near pines.

Uses: Beautiful in arrangements. ▶
Fine in flower borders and beds. Attractive in terrace pots.

Fragrant. Foliage and flowers are aromatic.

Cultural hints: Keep faded flowers trimmed off for continuous bloom.

POT MARIGOLD (*Calendula officinalis*). Composite Family
This is Shakespeare's Marigold, the "winking Mary-buds" of *Cymbeline*. Gerard writes, "Look wyslye on a Marigold" in the early morning to preserve you from "feveres" through the day! It is also reported that "some use to make their heyre yelo wyth the floure of this herbe not beyinge content with the natural color which God hath gyven them." In Holland, the dried petals are used to make broth. Alleviate a bee sting by rubbing a flower on the spot. In our gardens today these gay flowers (the heads up to four inches across) bring us sunshine on rainy days and dazzle the eye in pure sunlight. The ray flowers are in three or more ranks and often edged with a deeper tone. There are also completely double flowers that obscure the disk, and many intermediate forms, lending variety to the planting.

Height: 2 feet.

Color: Cream, lemon, gold, orange.

Location: Full sun, half sun.

Soil: Adapts to every soil, but prefers it light and sandy and moderately rich.

Planting: Sow in the open ground and transplant to stand ten inches apart. For earlier beginning of bloom, buy plants in the spring.

Uses: In bouquets. Group in the border for vivid color. The most cheerful of all flowers in the garden, terrace pots and planters.

Fragrant. Flower and foliage both have a pungent scent.

Cultural hints: Keep the faded flowers picked off for continuous bloom. ▶

NEMESIA (*N. strumosa*). Snapdragon Family
An unusual native of South Africa, not much grown in the U.S. The profuse cuplike flowers have appealing marked and bearded throats and come in three- to four-inch-wide clusters. Flourishes in a cool and damp climate. A fine rockery plant where summers are not hot and dry. The lance-shaped, sharply toothed leaves are attractive.

Height: 1 to 2 feet.

Color: White, yellow, bronze, pink, crimson, lavender. Usually very bright and rich tones.

Location: Sun, semishade, and open airy positions.

Soil: Rich earth. Give ample compost, also wood ashes.

Planting: Sow seeds indoors six weeks before the last frost. Set out young plants six inches apart. Handle carefully; seedlings are delicate.

Uses: Attractive for edgings and borders, and charming as cut flowers. Good in pots and planters.

Cultural hints: Feed during the summer at regular intervals for the finest display. ▼

PENSTEMON; BEARDED
TONGUE (*P. × gloxinioides*).
Snapdragon Family
There are many species of Penstemon,
all native to North America, most of
them in the West. Individual flowers
are like a small foxglove bloom. The
dramatic spires of nodding thimble-
shaped flowers are visited by hummingbirds. The name Penstemon
means "five stamens." This particular
variety is a hybrid of several species. It
comes in various colors; the glowing
red "Firebird" is superb.
HEIGHT: 18 to 24 inches.
COLOR: White, pink, lavender,
crimson, scarlet.
LOCATION: Open, sunny position.
SOIL: Deep, moist, well-drained
loam.
PLANTING: Sow indoors in February. Separate the seedlings to stand
twelve inches apart in the spring earth.
USES: Beautiful massed in the
border. A fine pot plant for the greenhouse. Excellent cut flowers, lasting
well in water. Not hardy in Northern
winters, but can be carried over in a
coldframe or greenhouse.
CULTURAL HINTS: Stake the
plants unobtrusively.
▼

▲

POPPY-MALLOW (*Callirhoe
digitata*). Mallow Family
Very rare, but do try it. Deeply cut
leaves and showy flowers are produced
in great profusion from early to late
summer. The plant will flourish at the
seashore in light, well-drained, sandy
soil, hot sun, and an open position.
Native from Missouri to Texas.
HEIGHT: To 2 feet.
COLOR: Violet to rosy-purple.
LOCATION: Full sun, open position, hot area.
SOIL: Light and sandy.
PLANTING: Sow seed in the open
ground where plants are to flower very
early in the spring—March, if possible.
Thin to stand twelve inches apart. Do
not transplant as the seedlings are too
delicate.
USES: An excellent and highly
decorative plant for the dry, sunny
border. Ideal for crevices in stone walls
and for dry banks.
CULTURAL HINTS: Staking is
necessary if there is much exposure to
wind.

PHYSALIS; CHINESE LANTERN
PLANT (*P. alkekengi*). Nightshade
Family
Originally from southeastern Europe to
Asia, where its fruits were used in
preserves. Sometimes called Ground-
cherry. Orange pods, like Chinese lan-
terns, follow inconspicuous flowers.

▲

Dried, it lasts all winter and makes a charming bouquet. Dry the stems in a horizontal position so the lanterns droop to the side for an Oriental festival effect. Eight berries with each change of the moon was an old-time cure for gout!

HEIGHT: To 2 feet.

COLOR: Vermilion.

LOCATION: Warm and sunny position.

SOIL: Light, sandy garden loam.

PLANTING: Sow early in the spring indoors. Set outdoors ten inches apart.

USES: Indoor winter decoration. Adds an exotic fall note to the garden where it grows.

CULTURAL HINTS: Stake the plants lest they tumble around the bed and the effect be lost. In warm climates this plant is perennial and can become a rampant weed.

PINCUSHION FLOWER (*Scabiosa atropurpurea*). Teasel Family

A native of southern Europe, Asia and Africa. I have seen mountainsides in the Swiss Alps covered with this plant. It produces showy compound flower heads. Silvery stamens resemble pins stuck in a cushion. A host to bees and butterflies all summer. The neat rosettes of leaves, deeply divided, are also appealing. The exotic seedpods are covered with bristly reddish hairs. The botanical name, *Scabiosa*, derives from the Latin, meaning "itch." It was said

▲

to cure various skin diseases and irritations.

HEIGHT: 18 to 30 inches.

COLOR: Lavender, black-purple, deep red, rose, white.

LOCATION: Full sunlight, open position.

SOIL: Fertile, well-drained soil, preferably alkaline.

PLANTING: Sow seed in the open ground where it is to grow, and separate seedlings to nine inches apart in the border. For earlier bloom, sow seed indoors in late March.

USES: Bouquets. A lovely bedding plant.

FRAGRANT. A delicate and sweet summer scent.

CULTURAL HINTS: Incorporate a little wood ash or lime in the soil around the plants during the growing season.

SAGE, SCARLET (*Salvia splendens*).
Mint Family
Native to Brazil, this is the reddest
flower there is. It blooms from August
to frost, in full sun. The flowers con-
sist of bracts, a large calyx and corolla,
all of dazzling scarlet. It is pollinated
by small birds attracted by the brilliant
color. The ancients used to whip up
the leaves with eggs, cream and flour;
they fried this batter and ate it to cure
backache.

▼

HEIGHT: 15 to 30 inches.
COLOR: Scarlet.
LOCATION: Full sun, open position.
SOIL: Fertile, well-drained soil.
PLANTING: Set out young plants
twelve inches apart in the spring,
grown from your own seed, sown indoors. Or else buy small nursery stock.
USES: Handsome in flower beds
and useful in foundation plantings.
Brings a note of intense color to an
indoor arrangement.
CULTURAL HINTS: To brighten
dull winter days, in October hang a few
bunches of blossoms upside down in a
cool airy place to dry and to use later
in a winter bouquet.

SALPIGLOSSIS; PAINTED
TONGUE (*S. sinuata*). Nightshade
Family
Exotic funnel-shaped flowers of velvet
texture and rich colors in designs like
a Paisley shawl. Delicate veining en-
hances their patterns. Don't be dis-
couraged by the spindly seedlings.
These take a sudden growing spurt, and
large trumpet-shaped flowers soon un-
fold and continue blooming until fall.
The plant originally came from Chile.
HEIGHT: 12 to 24 inches.
COLOR: Yellow, crimson, gold,
rose, blue, purple, lavender.
LOCATION: Full sun, protected
position. Needs a warm summer.
SOIL: Deep, rich, moist loam.
Unless soil is really fertile and good, do

▼

not try these beauties, for they will
only disappoint.
PLANTING: Start seeds early indoors, scattered on the surface of light
soil or in peat pellets to avoid transplanting shock. Set out young plants
ten inches apart.
USES: Excellent cut flowers. Fine
pot plants. Splendid in a cool greenhouse in winter.
CULTURAL HINTS: Insert a few
pieces of brushwood around the plants
as they grow to help support the slender
stems.

SATIN FLOWER; FAREWELL-TO-SPRING (*Godetia grandiflora*).
Evening-Primrose Family
Native to the western part of our country, but have become popular in parts of Europe, especially northern Italy, where they are favorite florists' flowers in spring and early summer. The blossoms, satin-petaled and cup-shaped, grow in a cluster along the upright stems.

HEIGHT: 9 to 18 inches.

COLOR: White, rose, scarlet, some with blotches of deeper or paler color.

LOCATION: Best where nights are cool and air is dry, with low humidity. Grow in light shade or full sun.

SOIL: Light, sandy loam, not too

▼

rich, slightly acid. If soil is too rich, the plant runs to foliage and flowers are scarce.

PLANTING: Sow seeds outdoors as soon as soil can be worked and in the border where they are to grow. Thin to stand eight inches apart. Does not transplant well.

USES: Lovely as cut flowers. Showy effect in the garden border. Flourishes in a cool greenhouse.

CULTURAL HINTS: Insert twiggy brush around the plants when they are half grown to help them stand up.

SNAPDRAGON (*Antirrhinum majus*).
Snapdragon Family
Among the most enchanting of all annuals for many reasons. One is the fun of watching a bumblebee light on the lower lip, swing it open, enter, and then back out pollen-covered. In Russia the plant was grown for its seed, which produced an edible oil. It was said that if you hung the dried flowers about your house you would be saved from being bewitched. Plants came originally from the Pyrenees and Mediterranean regions.

HEIGHT: 10 inches to 2 feet or higher.

COLOR: White, pink, red, yellow, purple.

LOCATION: Full sun, half sun.

SOIL: Rich loam.

PLANTING: Sow seeds outdoors in spring and transplant to stand eight inches apart. For earlier flowers, sow seed indoors or buy young seedlings to set out in the garden.

USES: Striking as cut flowers. Effective and lasting in the hardy border. Splendid for the greenhouse, forced into late-winter bloom.

FRAGRANT. Faintly scented.

CULTURAL HINTS: Pinch out the center stem of the seedlings so the plant will bush out. Stake the young growing plants for support.

▼

USES: Branches may be used in indoor arrangements if you sear the cut stems before putting them in water.

CULTURAL HINTS: Stake the growing stalks to prevent rain and wind from beating the plants down. Be careful in handling seedlings and later in cutting branches for bouquets as the sap may cause a temporary skin irritation.

▲

STAR OF THE DESERT (*Amberboa muricata*). Composite Family
Here is a rare yet easy-to-grow plant. Native to Spain and Morocco. The interesting leaves are jagged and the tiny flowers are all tubular in compact heads; no ray flowers. They begin to blossom sixteen weeks after seed is sown and continue in bloom until September. The flowers are borne on slender stems well above the foliage.

HEIGHT: 18 inches.

COLOR: White, purple, pink, violet.

LOCATION: Open, sunny position.

SOIL: Rich loam.

PLANTING: Sow the seeds in early March where they are to grow. Thin the young plants to stand nine inches apart.

USES: Appealing in the border and a fine cut flower.

FRAGRANT. Faintly scented.

CULTURAL HINTS: Keep faded flowers picked off for continuous bloom.

▲

SNOW-ON-THE-MOUNTAIN; GHOST WEED (*Euphorbia marginata*). Spurge Family
Cousin to the poinsettia. The upper leaves are interestingly margined with white. These are grown for the attractive foliage effect in the garden rather than for the small, insignificant flowers. Native to the Midwest of the United States, but has spread to Colorado, Texas and some eastern states.

HEIGHT: 1½ to 2½ feet.

COLOR: Gray-green and white.

LOCATION: Full sun and sheltered position.

SOIL: Adaptable to just about every soil, but prefers a light, sandy loam.

PLANTING: Sow seed in April-May where the plants are to grow, and thin out. Does not transplant well.

▲
STAR OF TEXAS (*Xanthisma texanum*). Composite Family
Native of Texas. The botanical name, from the Greek, means "dyed yellow," and indeed the flowers are so brilliant that they appear to have been dipped in a vat of molten gold. Attractive gray-green toothed foliage and two-inch-wide daisylike flowers. Thrives in a hot and dry climate, and blossoms from July to September.

HEIGHT: 18 to 30 inches.
COLOR: Yellow.
LOCATION: Sunny but protected position.
SOIL: Average or poor earth.
PLANTING: Sow seeds in the fall if your winters are mild; otherwise in the early spring where they are to grow. Thin to stand six inches apart.
USES: Sown in drifts, these plants will enhance a dry open space with dazzling color. Excellent for cut flowers.
CULTURAL HINTS: Stake the plants.

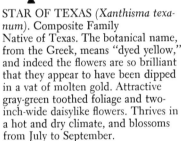

▲
STOCK (*Matthiola incana*) Mustard Family
A plant sometimes difficult to raise, but well worth a try for its handsome gray foliage and deeply scented flowers. Grows wild on the southern coast of the Isle of Wight and in the Mediterranean region. In Elizabethan times it was known as Stock Gilliflower because its perfume resembles that of the gilliflower or carnation.

HEIGHT: 12 to 30 inches.
COLOR: White, rose, crimson, purple, yellow.
LOCATION: Sun and an open, airy, cool position. Does especially well in a mountain environment where nights are fresh and cool.
SOIL: Rich loam, preferably with a little lime.
PLANTING: Sow seed indoors in late winter. Set out young plants in the spring.
USES: As a cut flower, Stocks fill the house with fragrance.
FRAGRANT. Spicy, lingering carnationlike scent, day and night.
CULTURAL HINTS: Stake the plants as unobtrusively as possible. Plant near the terrace or porch where the scent at night will be appreciated.

SUMMER (OR CAPE) FORGET-
ME-NOT (*Anchusa capensis* var.
'Blue Bird') Borage Family
A native of South Africa and now
naturalized in England. Tiny sky-blue
Forget-Me-Not blossoms grow in
clusters. When steeped in strong ale or
wine they are said to cure melancholy!
Anchusa, in Greek, means "dye."
Years ago a red dye from the roots was

▲

STRAWFLOWER; EVERLASTING
(*Helichrysum bracteatum*). Composite
Family
A plant from Australia, the home of
many Everlastings. Closely similar
species are native to Mediterranean
countries and Asia Minor. In ancient
Greece it was called the "Gods'
Flower" because at festival times the
statues of the gods were decorated with
garlands of these blossoms. It is grown
in Portugal and Spain, where it is used
dried to decorate the churches in
winter. In Italy many thousands of
bunches are sold every fall, particularly
to decorate the graves on All Saints
Day.
    HEIGHT: 2 feet.
    COLOR: White, yellow, crimson,
chestnut, rose. It is the tough involucral
bracts (surrounding the center, which
is the cluster of tiny true flowers) that
are so richly colored.
    LOCATION: Full sun.
    SOIL: Light, sandy soil, on the
dry side.
    PLANTING: Sow seeds where they
are to grow and transplant to stand
eight inches apart.
    USES: For fresh-cut flowers dur-
ing the summer, dried bouquets during
the winter.
    CULTURAL HINTS: To dry, cut
when half open, tie in bunches and
hang upside down in a cool, dark place
for a few weeks. In the garden, stake
the plants.

made into rouge and had many other
uses as well. This plant is a biennial in
warm climates.
    HEIGHT: 1½ to 2 feet.
    COLOR: Blue.
    LOCATION: Full sunlight or light
shade.
    SOIL: Moist, fertile soil.
    PLANTING: Sow seed in the open
ground in spring. Transplant to ten
inches apart. May also be sown indoors
at winter's end for earlier blooms.
    USES: Grow in drifts in borders
and beds, to emphasize their color.
Single specimens make charming pot
plants.
    CULTURAL HINTS: After the first
blooming, cut the plant back to about
eight inches and it will grow again and
be more beautiful and floriferous than
before.

SUNRAY; ROSE EVERLASTING
(*Helipterum roseum*). Composite
Family
From the midst of gray-green leaves
rise appealing flowers like double
daisies. The blossoms fold each night
and open wide again the next morning.
Most attractive in the garden as well as
in dried bouquets. Grows wild in
Australia and South Africa. Usually

▲

more delicate-looking and slightly
smaller than strawflowers (*Helichry-sum*).

    HEIGHT: 2 feet.
    COLOR: White or pink, with yellow centers. Of a crisp, taffeta-like texture.
    LOCATION: Full sun.
    SOIL: Light, sandy, dry soil.
    PLANTING: Sow seed in the open ground after the last frost. These are difficult to transplant, so thin to stand eight inches apart.
    USES: Good indoor winter decoration. Great addition to the mixed annual and perennial border.
    CULTURAL HINTS: To dry, cut the flowers before they are fully open. Hang the blossoms downward in a dry, airy space.

▲

SWEET SULTAN (*Centaurea moschata*). Composite Family
These plants reached England from Persia by way of Constantinople in the reign of Charles I, and have been garden favorites ever since. The fragrant shaggy flowers rise above deeply cut and toothed leaves; the foliage is as interesting as the blossoms. They last ten days or more indoors in water.
    HEIGHT: 2 feet.
    COLOR: Yellow, lavender, purple, white.
    LOCATION: Full sun.
    SOIL: Average earth.
    PLANTING: Sow in the open ground in spring; transplant the seedlings to stand six inches apart. May also be sown in the fall.
    USES: Blooms so readily and successfully that they are a fine flower for a child's garden or for a beginner. With these you just can't fail. Lovely in the border and as picked flowers.
    FRAGRANT. Sweet-scented.
    CULTURAL HINTS: Snip off dead blossom heads for a fine display and continuous bloom.

TALL

ANGEL'S TRUMPET; THORN-APPLE (*Datura metel*). Nightshade Family
Large, fragrant and beautiful white trumpets open all summer long. Prickly seedpods with green ruffs are curiously attractive. A sturdy, hairy, ranging plant, needing a lot of space, with large, gray-green markedly veined leaves. Naturalized from India, it flourishes in the tropics; it is especially prevalent in Guatemala and adjacent countries.

HEIGHT: To 4 feet.

COLOR: White inside and the upper edge rolled outward when in full bloom. Lower outer part violet or yellowish.

LOCATION: Full sun.

SOIL: Deep, rich, sandy loam.

PLANTING: Sow seeds indoors in late winter. Set seedlings out in the spring ten inches apart.

USES: Good in the cool greenhouse. Will fill a sunny corner in the garden and return year after year. Attractive in water indoors.

FRAGRANT. Deep, rich fragrance.

CULTURAL HINTS: Do not disturb the ground in the fall, and the self-sown seeds will sprout the next spring.

▼

BLACK-EYED-SUSAN VINE (*Thunbergia alata*). Acanthus Family
From tropical Africa, now naturalized in very warm parts of other continents. Attractive, neat, trim blossoms, one to two inches across, appear to be cut from crisp tissue paper. The plant, with its cheerful flowers and slender twining stems, grows to six or seven feet. For a more compact plant, pinch back the growing tips.

HEIGHT: A vine, 6 to 7 feet high.

COLOR: Orange, yellow, white, with jet-black eyes.

LOCATION: Full sun, sheltered position.

SOIL: Moist, rich, well-drained soil.

PLANTING: Sow seeds indoors in February or early March in a sunny window or greenhouse, or outdoors when the earth is warm and nights are frost-free. Thin to six inches apart, and set in individual pots until May, then in their outdoor location. If you set out young plants you will have blooms sooner.

USES: Hanging baskets, window boxes, rock gardens, ground cover. Splendid for the greenhouse, where it will flourish for months on end.

CULTURAL HINTS: Provide a string or trellis for the vine to climb on.

▼

BUTTERFLY FLOWER;
POOR-MAN'S ORCHID
(*Schizanthus pinnatus*). Nightshade
Family
Lipped flower with spotted and
blotched petals somewhat resembles
a small butterfly. An interesting plant
from Chile with a pale green foliage.
The name derives from the Greek:
schizo means "to split," and *anthos*,
"flower"—this description refers to the
petals of the blossoms, which are deeply
cleft. The plant thrives where nights
are cool and days do not get too hot.
HEIGHT: 2 to 4 feet.
COLOR: White, rose, yellow,
pink, purple.
LOCATION: Sun, light shade.
Sheltered position.
SOIL: Moist garden loam.
PLANTING: Sow indoors in late
winter. Set out in spring after danger
of frost is past, one foot apart. Plant
in succession to extend the blossoming
season.
USES: Effective in the flower
border because of their abundance of
bloom. Appropriate for window boxes
and hanging baskets, the gaily
colored and deeply cut flowers tumble
over the rims.
CULTURAL HINTS: Give ample
water during the growing season.
These plants are difficult in Northern
gardens, and they have a rather short,
though spectacular, season of bloom,
so they may need later replacement by
other plants.

CANARY-BIRD VINE (*Tropaeolum
peregrinium*). Nasturtium Family
A well-loved climbing plant originally
found near Lima, Peru, in the
eighteenth century, it grows wild in
Peru today. It bears interestingly
shaped fringed yellow flowers with
green spurs. They suggest a scattered
flock of canaries in flight, and are
produced from July to October. Leaves
are round but deeply lobed.
HEIGHT: Stems about 8 feet long.
COLOR: Canary-yellow.
LOCATION: Open, sunny position,
or part shade.
SOIL: Average garden loam,
slightly moist.
PLANTING: Seeds are best sown
indoors to get a head start. Can be
sown in April or May where they are
to flower. In either case, set out or thin
out to stand nine inches apart.
USES: Makes a beautiful screen
planting. Grows in the greenhouse.
The flowers are lovely in a small bouquet because of the scent. Used as a
garnish or in salads, they have a
tangy cress flavor.
FRAGRANT. Sweet-scented.
CULTURAL HINTS: Give a trellis
or strings to climb on. Does best where
summers are cool and night temperatures drop below 65 degrees.

▲

CONEFLOWER *(Rudbeckia bicolor)*.
Composite Family
Each blossom has a high, cone-shaped
center. Easy, rewarding and adaptable
—good for beginners. This annual
comes from Texas, where it runs wild
along the highways for miles on end,
blooming in late summer and autumn.
Flower heads are two inches across,
and wider in garden forms. Seeds are
well liked by finches. The genus is
named for two botany professors called
Rudbeck, father and son.

HEIGHT: 2 to 3 feet.
COLOR: Orange, yellow, ma-
hogany; the disk black or very dark red.
LOCATION: Thrives in hot, dry,
sunny spot. Open, airy position.
SOIL: Adapts to almost every soil.
PLANTING: Sow seeds in the open
ground in the spring. Separate seedlings to stand six inches apart.
USES: Splendid for cutting. A
striking plant in the border.
CULTURAL HINTS: Stake the
young plants to keep upright in wind
and rain.

COREOPSIS; CALLIOPSIS
(Coreopsis tinctoria). Composite
Family
Feathery foliage with finely cut leaves
bends and ripples in the breeze.
Native to our plains states, these are
surprisingly strong plants that you
can't keep down. The often bicolored

flowers are very conspicuous. They
will grow in towns as they are fairly
impervious to smoky air. *Coreopsis*,
from the Greek, means "like a bed
bug," and is suggested by the color and
shape of the seeds. These were formerly used to dye cloth.

HEIGHT: To 3 feet; also dwarf
forms to 9 inches.
COLOR: Golden-yellow, polished
mahogany, velvety crimson-brown.
LOCATION: Full sun and open,
airy position.
SOIL: Adapts to almost all soils.
PLANTING: Sow seed in the open
ground in the spring. Transplant to
twelve inches apart.
USES: Excellent bedding plants.
Fine for cut flowers.
CULTURAL HINTS: Before they
grow too tall, stake the young plants
to keep them upright in wind and
storms.

▼

COCKSCOMB; WOOLFLOWER

(*Celosia argentea*). Amaranthus Family
Native to Asian tropics. Some flower
heads are heavily crested (variety
cristata); others are like ostrich plumes
of shiny silken texture. Because of
the lasting quality, both in the garden
and indoors, the plant symbolizes
longevity. This plant is popular in
Central America, where it is used
extensively in flower beds and parks.
Reliable and easy to grow. A dramatic
flower that may be dried for winter
bouquets.

HEIGHT: 2 to 4 feet.
COLOR: Red, yellow, orange, gold.
LOCATION: Sun and half sun,
sheltered position. Will tolerate a
hot, dry climate.
SOIL: Deep, rich, well-drained
earth.
PLANTING: Sow seeds in the open
ground in the spring, or indoors in
March, close to the window. Transplant indoor seedlings into three-inch
pots, and later move plants outdoors to
stand eight inches apart only when
weather is settled.
USES: Dry for winter bouquets.
Fine in beds and in summer flower
arrangements.
CULTURAL HINTS: To dry, cut the
flowers at their peak and hang them
in bunches upside-down in a shady,
airy place.

COSMOS (*C. bipinnatus*). Composite
Family
An old-fashioned favorite that flourished in our grandmothers' gardens. A
good annual today for all of us—
especially for a child's garden, because
of the ease and rapidity with which
the plant grows and flowers and the
long season of bloom. It is, in fact, an
encouraging plant for beginners of
all ages. Lacy foliage is most delicate
and attractive. The airy, wide-petaled
but thin-textured flowers, with their
gold centers, make delightful bouquets.
HEIGHT: To 4 feet or higher.
Seedsmen sell various kinds.
COLOR: Red, rose, lavender,
white, orange, yellow.
LOCATION: Full sun or partial
shade.
SOIL: Adapts to every soil. Best
fairly dry and not too rich.
PLANTING: Sow in the open
ground in the spring. Separate feathery
seedlings to stand twelve inches apart.
USES: Beautiful in bouquets.
Stately at the back of the border.
CULTURAL HINTS: For a continuous abundance of large flowers, feed
wood ashes or small amounts of a
commercial fertilizer when the buds
first appear. Stake the young and
growing plants.

▲

CUP-AND-SAUCER VINE (*Cobaea scandens*). Phlox Family
A rampant climber from Mexico that will reach twenty feet in height. Thrives in both sun and shade. The curling tendrils and seedpods are as pretty as the large, swinging bell-shaped flowers. Each blossom is like a cup in a saucer of green foliage.
HEIGHT: A vine, to 20 feet, and to 40 feet in the South.
COLOR: Purple, lavender, white.
LOCATION: Full sun, partial sun, sheltered position.
SOIL: Adapts to every variety but prefers it light and sandy.
PLANTING: Plant seed (each seed on its edge) indoors in March. Set seedlings out in May to stand eighteen inches to two feet apart.
USES: Covers walls, trails over fences, climbs trellises.
CULTURAL HINTS: Provide a trellis, string or wire for the tendrils to grasp.

CYPRESS VINE; STAR GLORY (*Quamoclit pennata*). Morning Glory Family
Native to tropical South America, this is another climber, often reaching a height of fifteen feet. Does especially well in the southern and western parts of the United States. Finely divided delicate leaves, and scarlet, vermilion or white flowers from June to September. Attracts hummingbirds.
HEIGHT: To 15 feet or more.
COLOR: Scarlet, vermilion, white.
LOCATION: Full sun, partial shade, sheltered position.
SOIL: Rich, sandy loam.
PLANTING: Sow seeds indoors in winter. Soak the seeds overnight in lukewarm water to soften the hard shell before planting. Set seedlings out in the spring one foot apart.
USES: Covers fences, walls, the side of a house, garage, barn, arbors, pergolas and porch walls.
CULTURAL HINTS: Give string or a trellis to climb on.

FLOWERING TOBACCO (*Nicotiana alata*). Nightshade Family
The whole house will be fragrant in the evening from one bouquet of these starry white flowers. Plant near the porch or terrace so you will be able to appreciate them on summer nights. An added asset: The plant attracts unusual and beautiful noc-

turnal moths—be sure to watch for them. Blossoms droop in the sun and expand late in the day (a few horticultural forms remain open all day). Comes from South America, the Pacific Islands, Australia.

HEIGHT: 2 to 3½ feet.
COLOR: White, red.
LOCATION: Full sun, half shade.
SOIL: Adapts to almost every kind of earth.
PLANTING: Sow in the open ground. Separate to stand eight inches apart. For earlier bloom, sow indoors in February and set out in the spring. Or buy young plants from a nursery.
USES: Splendid in large clumps in the border. Lovely in indoor bouquets.
FRAGRANT. Deeply scented, especially in the evening.

▼

CULTURAL HINTS: Do not disturb the earth where plants grow, as they reseed.

▲

FOUR-O'CLOCK; MARVEL OF PERU (*Mirabilis jalapa*). Four O'Clock Family
From South America and Mexico. Tubular flowers open at about four in the afternoon and stay open all night and the next day, too, if it is rainy or dark. Brilliant sun causes them to fold up. These are perennials in the tropics; annuals where winters are cold. In France, they are called Belle de Nuit. This old-fashioned plant deserves more attention today.

HEIGHT: 2 to 3½ feet.
COLOR: Red, yellow, violet, white.
LOCATION: Full sun.
SOIL: Well-drained, average soil.
PLANTING: Sow indoors six weeks before the last frost. Space the plants one foot apart.
USES: Your garden will have a new look each afternoon when these blossoms open.
CULTURAL HINTS: Keep well watered. In the fall you can dig up the tuberous roots and store over the winter. Fresh plants will come from these the following season—plants with larger flowers.

HONESTY; MOONWORT *(Lunaria annua)*. Mustard Family
From southeast Europe and west Asia. Seeds are visible through translucent silvery roundish papery pods, hence the ▶ name *Lunaria*. These unusual pods are extremely decorative indoors. The roots may be eaten in salads.

HEIGHT: 2 to 3½ feet.
COLOR: Flowers are purple to red.
LOCATION: Filtered sun.
SOIL: Average garden loam or rather poor, dry soil; grow in part shade.
PLANTING: Sow indoors in March and set seedlings out in the spring nine inches apart.
USES: The seedpods make an attractive all-winter dried arrangement. These should be gathered as soon as ripe, and in dry weather. Flowers in the summer are excellent and fragrant in indoor bouquets.
FRAGRANT. Sweet-scented.
CULTURAL HINTS: Do not disturb the ground where plants grow. Seeds fallen to earth will sprout and bloom abundantly the following season. The plant is really a biennial.

▲

JOB'S-TEARS *(Coix lacryma-jobi)*. Grass Family
This is a broad-leafed tropical grass. Grown for the hard-shelled beadlike seeds about half an inch long that develop in drooping clusters. Dry these for winter bouquets. In olden days the "beads" were strung and used for teething babies. The plant is the source of a cereal food in parts of tropical Asia, where it is endemic. Perennial in warm climates.
HEIGHT: 2 to 4 feet.
COLOR: Seeds are white, pearl-gray or dark gray.
LOCATION: Full sun.
SOIL: Average garden loam.
PLANTING: Sow indoors in winter. Set out in the spring one foot apart. Soak the seeds for twenty-four hours before sowing.

USES: Fascinating additions to dried bouquets. Interesting grown in a clump toward the back of the border.
CULTURAL HINTS: Stake the plants. To dry, hang the stems in a cool, airy place. Stand upright if curved stems are desired; hang upside-down if you want straight stems.

LARKSPUR *(Delphinium ajacis)*. Buttercup Family
A native of southern Europe. Spires of petaled flowers rise from soft, feathery, brilliant green foliage. If kept trimmed, it blooms until frost. The Greeks, who liked dolphins, originally gave it its botanical name. In the unfolding buds tossing in the breeze, they saw dolphins tossing in the sea spray, and

▲

so called it *delphinion*, the Greek word
for dolphin. The epithet *ajacis* came
about because, according to classical
legend, the plant was reputed to
have sprung from the blood of the hero
Ajax. The juice of the flowers, mixed
with water, was said to strengthen the
sight.

HEIGHT: 2 to 4 feet; a dwarf
strain to 1 foot.

COLOR: Pink, blue, purple, white.

LOCATION: Sun, filtered sun; the
plant does best in cooler places.

SOIL: Adapts to nearly every soil,
but prefers soil that is fertile, moist
and well drained.

PLANTING: Sow seeds outdoors
in the fall or in March. Fall seeding
brings earlier flowers as well as taller
flower spikes. Thin to stand eight
inches apart. Does not transplant well.

USES: Splendid growing along
wall or fence. Beautiful in bouquets.
Conspicuous flowers are effective in
clumps in the flower border.

CULTURAL HINTS: Trim off dead
flowers for continuing bloom. Stake
the plants.

LOVE-LIES-BLEEDING
(*Amaranthus caudatus*). Amaranthus
Family

The botanical name, *Amaranthus*,
from the Greek, means "does not
wither." Sometimes known as Tassel
Flower. The blossoms are everlasting.
The terminal spiked clusters of blooms
droop in long tassels like ropes of
chenille. A favorite in tropical gardens.
Flowers from July to September.

HEIGHT: 2 to 6 feet.

COLOR: Dark red to red-brown;
in one variety, green.

LOCATION: Full sun.

SOIL: Thrives in dry heat and
poor soil.

PLANTING: Sow in the open
ground. Transplants easily. Set to stand
eighteen inches apart.

USES: Long-lasting flowers in the
garden. Tall enough to be used as a
screen planting at the borders of
terraces.

CULTURAL HINTS: Stake the
plants.

▼

▲

AFRICAN MARIGOLD *(Tagetes erecta)*. Composite Family
Native from Mexico to Argentina, the word "African" was possibly once a seed dealer's sales gimmick. A stiff, sturdy plant, and a most agreeable flower for beginners and children to grow, as well as for more sophisticated gardeners. Lasts weeks indoors, bringing sunshine with it. Named for Tages, grandson of Jupiter, a demigod celebrated for his beauty.

HEIGHT: 2 to 3½ feet.

COLOR: Orange, lemon-yellow, white.

LOCATION: Open, sunny location.

SOIL: Light, well-drained, moderately rich.

PLANTING: Sow seeds in the open ground in May and transplant seedlings to stand ten inches apart. To hasten the flowering season, buy young plants or plant seeds indoors in late winter.

USES: Dazzling bouquets. Attractive grouped in the flower bed. Thrives in pots on terraces.

FRAGRANT. The foliage has a pungent odor.

CULTURAL HINTS: Stake young plants. Keep withered flower heads picked off for continuous bloom.

MORNING GLORY *(Ipomoea rubro-coerulea* var. 'Heavenly Blue').
Morning Glory Family
A beautiful sky-blue flower whose blossoms unfurl from red buds each morning to greet the sun. Will bloom around a window frame if given cord to climb on. Because of their white centers the flowers have a wide-eyed look. Blooms from June to the first frost, if started indoors; from August on, if started in May-out-of-doors.

HEIGHT: A vine—to 10 feet.

COLOR: Buds red, flowers blue.

LOCATION: Sunny, sheltered position.

SOIL: Average garden soil, on the dry side.

PLANTING: Notch the hard-shelled seeds with a file, or soak overnight. Plant a half inch deep indoors in individual peat pots at winter's end. Set the little pots in the ground six inches apart. Does not survive transplanting when the soil is loosened from the roots. May also be sown in the garden in spring.

USES: Window boxes, planters. Will grow up a wall, fence or trellis, summerhouses or posts, where they form a screen planting.

CULTURAL HINTS: Remove fading flowers to increase the number of blooms.

▼

▲

MOONFLOWER (*Calonyction
aculeatum*). Morning Glory Family
From tropical America, and perennial
in quite warm climates. Grow near
your porch or terrace so you can watch
the four- to six-inch-wide fragrant satiny
flowers open rapidly at dusk. They
gleam in the moonlight and starlight
and remain open until noon the
following day, when they fold up. The
attractive leaves are large and heart-
shaped. Growth and bloom best in a
long, warm summer.

HEIGHT: A vine—to 20 feet.

COLOR: White, often with
greenish central lines.

LOCATION: Full sun.

SOIL: Average garden loam, not
too rich, or the plant runs to foliage.

PLANTING: Sow indoors in individual peat pots, one seed to a pot,
first notching the hard-shelled seeds
with a file or soaking overnight to
hasten germination. Plant pots and all
in the open ground in May, nine inches
apart. Do not disturb the roots. Give
ample water all summer.

USES: Charming for covering a
lattice, fence or trellis. An excellent
screen planting.

FRAGRANT. Very sweet scent.

CULTURAL HINTS: Give wire or
string to climb on.

NASTURTIUM *(Tropaeolum majus).*
Nasturtium Family
Grows wild from Mexico to Chile. A
popular, beloved flower grown by
everyone's grandmother, and also found
today in the most modern of gardens.
Blooms in a vast array of colors. May
be single or double, and comes up to
two and one-half inches across. The
tiny leaves resemble the shield of a
medieval knight. They are delicious in
salads; the taste is similar to watercress.

HEIGHT: Climbing form to four
feet, and dwarf 'Tom Thumb' form to
one foot.

COLOR: All the tawny orange,
yellow, red shades. Also creamy white,
salmon, scarlet, mahogany.

LOCATION: Open, sunny spot.

SOIL: Hot and dry sandy earth,
poor in nutrients. Blooms are sparse if
soil is rich.

PLANTING: Sow outdoors three-
quarters of an inch deep where they are
to grow. Space the bush varieties six
inches apart—the climbers ten inches.

USES: Will grow low in the
border, or climb a low fence, stumps,
rocks, blooming as it goes. Popular cut
flowers.

CULTURAL HINTS: Treat these
plants roughly for best results. Do not
water unless in a really dry spell. Do not
feed, or they will run to foliage and
blooms will be limited. For attacks of
black aphids, spray with Black Leaf 40.

▼

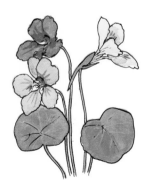

For bouquets, pick early in the morning when the flowers begin to open. Promptly seal the cut stems by dipping in boiling water.

CULTURAL HINTS: Grow where plants are protected from wind.

SALVIA; MEALYCUP SAGE
(*S. farinacea* var. 'Blue Bedder').
Mint Family

Originally from Texas, this plant has gray-green leaves from four to six inches long, and spikes of violet-blue flowers. In mild climates it often comes up the second year, but is best treated as an annual. Provides abundant color in the garden in late summer and fall. Somewhat resembles lavender with its wands of half-inch-long blooms along a silvery-white stem.

HEIGHT: 2 to 3 feet.
COLOR: Violet-blue.
LOCATION: Open, sunny position.
SOIL: Deep, rich, light loam.
PLANTING: Sow seed indoors before winter's end. Set out in the garden in May, twelve inches apart.
USES: Excellent as a cut flower. Dries well for winter arrangements. Appealing when grown in the flower border in groups of three or five interspersed among slightly lower-growing plants with white or yellow flowers.
FRAGRANT. Subtle scent.
CULTURAL HINTS: Stake the plants when in an exposed position.

POPPY, SHIRLEY (*Papaver rhoeas*).
Poppy Family

This is a strain of the common red Poppy often found in grainfields in Europe, the Flanders Field Poppy. The flowers are dazzling in the summer sunlight. Appealing crinkled silky blooms are not long-lasting, but they are produced in profusion during the summer months.

HEIGHT: 2 to 3 feet.
COLOR: Pink, carmine, scarlet, crimson, white.
LOCATION: Hot and sunny spot.
SOIL: Light, sandy loam, well-drained.
PLANTING: Sow in the open ground where they are to grow. Do not transplant seedlings but thin to stand six inches apart. If sown in the autumn will bloom earlier.
USES: Effective covering sunny slopes or grown in drifts in the border.

▲

SNOWCUP (*Anoda lavateroides*).
Mallow Family
Originally from Texas and Mexico.
Seldom grown, but not difficult. Arrow-shaped leaves with two-inch flowers in the leaf axils. These plants make a fine hedge for a season, blooming from July to September.
  HEIGHT: 4 feet.
  COLOR: Purple, violet, white.
  LOCATION: Full sun.
  SOIL: Garden loam, a little on the heavy side and not too dry.
  PLANTING: Sow seed in the open ground as soon as danger of frost is over. Transplant to stand eighteen inches apart.
  USES: Splendid for the back of a border, good for a hedge.
  CULTURAL HINTS: Water during dry spells in summer, and especially after young plants are first set out.

▲

SPIDERFLOWER (*Cleome spinosa*).
Caper Family
From the West Indies. Long-stemmed stamens and pistils exserted from the large, airy blossom give a spidery effect. Leaves are large, composed of long narrow leaflets. There are spines at the base of each leaf and on the stem. Blooms three months after seed is sown, and flowers freely from June to August. When the blooms fade, decorative curved seedpods like spider legs develop and radiate from the ripened ovary.
  HEIGHT: 3 to 5 feet.
  COLOR: Pink, white, lavender.
  LOCATION: A dry, sunny spot. Will tolerate some shade.
  SOIL: Average garden loam.
  PLANTING: Sow seeds indoors in March and set plants out in May, spacing about eighteen inches apart.
  USES: Good background planting, particularly along a fence or wall.
  FRAGRANT. Pungent scent, to many people not pleasing.
  CULTURAL HINTS: Stake young plants.

SUNFLOWER *(Helianthus annuus).*
Composite Family
In Central America and Peru this
flower was the emblem of the Sun God
and often depicted on ancient Inca
Temples. When the Mormons headed
west from Missouri, all across the
plains the men dropped Sunflower
seeds. The next summer, wagons
carrying the women and children had
only to follow the Sunflower trails. In
Russia, Argentina and other countries
the plant is raised commercially for the
oil in the seeds, which is processed into
salad and cooking oils, and, under heat,
into oil for soap, paint, margarine.

HEIGHT: 5 to 10 feet.

COLOR: Yellow.

LOCATION: Full sun, part shade.

SOIL: Average garden loam. Does
well also in dry, poor soil.

▼

PLANTING: Sow in the open
ground in spring. Transplant seedlings
to stand eighteen to twenty-four inches
apart.

USES: As a temporary hedge or
screen. Produces seeds to feed the
winter birds, especially goldfinches,
cardinals and many others. Squirrels
greatly relish the seeds, as do also many
humans in Russia, Central Asia and
China. A great favorite, too, of health
food enthusiasts in this country. A
dramatic accent in the garden, particularly when grown in a clump apart
in some vacant space, or in a not too
rigid line against the southern side of
a fence or wall.

CULTURAL HINTS: Stake with
stout canes.

SWEET PEA *(Lathyrus odoratus).*
Pea Family
Airy blossoms with ruffled, wavy petals
that come in many tints and shades. A
climbing plant with leaves terminating
in curling tendrils. One of the sweetest-
scented of all annuals. The fragrance is
especially strong at dusk and after a
rain. Indoors, the delicious odor fills
the house from a bouquet in one room.
Although from Italy (and grows even
as far south as Sicily), sweet peas
flourish best in a cool, moist climate.

HEIGHT: Climbs 4 to 8 feet.
There are also nonclimbing bush varieties available from many seedsmen.

COLOR: Mostly pale to middle-
value pinks, blues, lavender, but also
some intense orange and red to deep
red and violet.

LOCATION: Full sun.

SOIL: Deep, rich soil, slightly
alkaline.

PLANTING: Soak seeds overnight
to speed germination. Sow them outdoors in mid-March or early April, two
inches apart—no need to thin or transplant seedlings. Helpful if the planting
soil has been prepared the previous fall.

USES: Excellent for cutting.
Splendid to grow in a cool greenhouse.

FRAGRANT. Very fragrant.

CULTURAL HINTS: A deep mulch of manure or compost benefits the roots and keeps them cool. Hoeing the surface between rows also keeps the under-soil cool. Give wire or string to climb on. Best grown in a bed apart from the flower garden proper. See also CULTURAL HINTS under LUPINE, page 40.

TITHONIA (T. rotundifolia). Composite Family
From Central and South America, Mexico and the West Indies. Golden flower of the Incas. Dramatic tall stalks covered with glowing three-inch blossoms form a fine background planting. Blooms from mid-July to real frost.
HEIGHT: 6 feet.
COLOR: Red-orange above, gold underneath.
LOCATION: Full sun.
SOIL: Average garden loam.
PLANTING: Sow in the open ground in May. Transplant seedlings to

two feet apart. For a longer summer of flowers, sow seeds indoors in late March.
USES: Fine cut flower if you sear the stems and set in a deep vase of lukewarm water. A temporary hedge, a most welcome screen, and a good background planting.
CULTURAL HINTS: Stake the growing plants. Needs plenty of water in dry weather, because of its great size.

COMMON ZINNIA (Z. elegans).
Composite Family
From tropical America. Dahlia-like flowers to four inches across, with slightly reflexed petals and a convex disk. Among the brightest, most cheerful of all annuals. The dazzling colors are unsurpassed in brilliance and variety of tints and tones. (See also pages 30, 31, 64.)
HEIGHT: 2 to 3½ feet.
COLOR: Every color but blue.
LOCATION: Full sun.
SOIL: Well-drained, moderately rich soil.
PLANTING: Sow seed in the open ground. Space to stand one foot apart. For earlier bloom start seed indoors in late March and plant out only when large enough to readily handle.
USES: Effective and showy in masses in the flower border or in a separate bed. Excellent as cut flowers.
CULTURAL HINTS: Needs no special care, but keep faded flowers picked off and water well in dry weather.

▼

▼

▲

ZINNIA, FANTASY HYBRIDS.
Composite Family
Shaggy, tousled loose flowers up to five
inches across. Some petals are quilled,
others are loose and twisted. These
Zinnias come in both pastel tones and
brilliant hues. Zinnias, are for adults
and children alike—for children, especially, because they are so easy to raise,
grow fast and produce an abundance
of flowers all summer.

HEIGHT: 2 to 3 feet or more.
COLOR: Every color but blue.
LOCATION: Full sun.
SOIL: Moderately rich, well-
drained soil.
PLANTING: Sow in the spring
where they are to bloom. Thin to stand
ten inches apart. Or buy seedlings to
hasten the blooming period.
USES: Wonderful massed in the
flower border. Excellent cut flowers.
CULTURAL HINTS: Pick off wilted
flower heads for continuous bloom.
Stake the plants if they grow over thirty
inches high.

▲

**ZINNIA, CALIFORNIA GIANT
HYBRID.** Composite Family
A really superb strain, large-flowered,
long-stemmed. In appearance they
resemble Decorative Dahlias. As dried
flowers, they hold their vivid colors.

HEIGHT: 2 to 3 feet or more.
COLOR: Tints and shades of every
color but blue.
LOCATION: Full sun.
SOIL: Well-drained garden loam.
PLANTING: Sow seed in the open
ground; space twelve inches apart. Or
buy young plants from a nursery to
prolong the blooming season.
USES: For massing in the flower
border. For cut flowers. For drying.
CULTURAL HINTS: Stake the
plants. Trim off dead heads for continuous bloom. Wood ashes are beneficial.

2. Annuals, the Easiest Flowers of All

Annuals are the flowers that grow from seed to flower to seed again in a single season. They are varied and colorful, prolific and long-lasting. Most of them, once they begin to bloom, keep right on until frost, some even a little beyond. To plant an annual garden you begin in the spring with a piece of inviting black earth. There is something clearcut about annuals: each year you start with a fresh slate, so to speak; you replan, think up a different color scheme and begin anew.

We invariably plant too many annuals; in our garden they grow in a real tangle, but we enjoy the rich profusion of color, fragrance and beauty. We can pick from early summer to frost. Here we like to wander on a sunny morning or at dusk, and here we pause to watch butterflies and hummingbirds gather nectar. Here we also listen—to the various sounds of summer, including one of the finest, which weaves through all the others—the purring hum of honeybees as they hover over the blooms.

Here is a choice of four different annual gardens that provide fun, satisfaction, and flowers all season. The first is a garden 12 feet by 4 feet consisting of familiar varieties. The second is a small corner garden 6 feet by 6 feet. The third is a free-form curving border filled with easy-to-grow but unusual flowers—with annuals rather unfamiliar to most of us. The fourth, also 12 feet by 4 feet, is made up of flowers to hang and dry for bouquets to enjoy all winter long.

If you are new to gardens and gardening, annuals are a fine introduction—and an inexpensive one. They do beautifully in average garden soil. A variety of locations will please them. Annuals will thrive along a fence, a wall, edging a drive, in a separate bed by themselves, and as a follow-up in an area of spring bulbs. These versatile plants flourish almost anywhere as long they they have sun. Nearly all annuals make one insistent demand: plenty of sun—full, unfiltered sun—all day, straight and strong.

Starting from scratch, to turn a piece of lawn into a flower garden, you first mark out a plan on the grass—with sticks and string if it is to be symmetrical, with a garden hose if you want curves. Any size and shape will do. A space twelve feet by four feet is a good proportion, an area in which you will be able to grow a number of varieties and have a rainbow of flowers from June to November.

With size and shape determined, and when all danger of frost is past, you can dig and prepare for seeding. Spade the earth, remove roots and rocks, and, after shaking off the earth still clinging to it, toss out the sod. Spread and turn in fertilizer, preferably of an organic nature. (Organic plant food continues to enrich the soil over a long period.) Should the ground already be dug, merely add plant food and spade up the area thoroughly.

The time to sow seed is usually in April (or early May in the North), when leaves everywhere are unfolding. When your seedlings come up through the ground, pushing twin pale-green leaves before them, you will realize that you probably have more than you can use. This is fine for two reasons: you can share with neighbors; also, a few plants usually succumb to cutworms and others to mysterious unidentified ailments or invaders. So it is wise to have extra plants.

Should you get a late start in the spring and June has arrived before you know it, and you still want an annual garden, there is a quick, lazy way to have it. Simply purchase small annual plants from the local nursery. The advantage of this is the speed with which you obtain a flowering garden. Many of the tiny seedlings in their individual pots are already in bloom or near it. Buying annuals is also invaluable if you have rented a house for the summer and want flowers in a hurry. The disadvantages are that it costs more, and you cannot always get the varieties and colors you want. If you set out plants, be sure to wait until night frosts are definitely past, or your plants will be damaged or killed.

I would like to introduce you briefly to the annuals in the first two gardens that follow. The low-growing border plants include Flossflower (*Ageratum*), a furry flower lovely to feel as well as to look at; Lobelia, another blue that is sometimes an electric shade, and often has a tiny, sparkling white eye. The foliage is soft and fernlike, with a metallic sheen. In all the tawny shades comes the fresh-scented, low-growing Nasturtium, with its fine, crinkly seedpods that follow the flowers. The appealing round green leaves, when young and tender, are fine in salads. Dwarf Phlox brings to the garden pinks, reds, white, and scarlet; and it never stops flowering until frost. Verbena grows in brilliant shades of red, deep ink-blue, pink, lavender, and purple. Its wanderlust will not let it stay primly and properly in one spot, like the Phlox and most of the others; the flower heads reach out beyond the border that would confine them. This is an adventurous flower.

Among the best of the border plants are Dwarf Zinnias; 'Persian Carpet' is a variety that opens in shades of cream, orange, yellow, and deep mahogany, with pointed petals tipped a contrasting tone. They invite irresistible tiny bouquets on bedside tables and dressers, and in bathrooms. These little flowers prove that the tall and the big are not always the most rewarding.

Of middle-to-tall height is the plumed Cockscomb (Celosia argentea). The plumed blossoms resemble graceful bunches of windblown wool caught loosely together on a stem. The white Stock, with spikes of close-crowded wide-open flowers, has a spicy fragrance. Also for the middle of the larger bed is Baby's Breath (Gypsophila), with tiny, delicate, airy flowers making sprays of white mist. The Pincushion Flower (Scabiosa), does, indeed, look like a pincushion stuck with pins. White, pink, red, and lavender blossoms wave in the breeze on top of slender green stalks—a great addition to any bouquet, as well as your garden.

Among the medium-to-tall annuals are dwarf Dahlias, with firm, tawny blossoms in red, pink, yellow, and flame. One of their charms is that the flower petals may be eaten in salad. No matter how this idea strikes you, at least they would handsomely decorate any summer salad bowl. Another of the advantages of Dahlias is that by fall they have produced new tubers. These may be saved for the next subsequent year. After frost, dig and store tubers for the winter in ordinary garden soil in a cool, but not freezing, place. By spring, replant for another season of even more flowers—an economical arrangement.

Tall Giant Zinnias, also in autumn colors, are sturdy, attractive and dramatic, flowering as they do from July to frost. Equally striking are the brilliant Marigolds. Both Marigolds and Zinnias last many days in indoor bouquets.

Tithonia, the golden flower of the Incas, is a spectacular flower.

Though it wanders wild over the mountain slopes of Peru, flaunting its rich flaming orange, it will also, even lacking the Inca influence, thrive among the annuals in your garden.

The third garden—the garden of the unusual annuals—is a place of surprises. Though the catalog names of these flowers may be unfamiliar, their appearance and ways make them most tempting. They are as easy to grow as the better-known varieties. If you want something new and different for yourself and your friends to see, this third one is for you.

In the fourth garden, the colorful blooms not only spend the summer with you but the whole long winter as well. Recently, gardeners have developed a new enthusiasm for an old-fashioned custom: dried flowers have come into their own. The flowers of this garden can be made into gay and brilliant bouquets that last almost indefinitely. These flowers may be arranged with seedpods, dried goldenrod and such, which you can readily find in the autumn fields and along the roadsides. You can even twine a few dried flowers into your Christmas door wreath to enhance it.

Have you a warm, dark place—a closet, cupboard or attic, perhaps? That is all you need. Pick the flowers when no moisture is on them, when each one is perfect, insect-free, and not fully opened (the petals cling better before being completely expanded). Strip off all foliage, hang heads down in clusters in the dark, warm place of your choice. If it is a closet or cupboard, open the door occasionally for circulation of air.

To experiment further, try Marigolds, Dahlias, Zinnias, and other blooms from any of the other three gardens or from any part of your outdoors. For these, use the following procedure: Select a box with a tight bottom—wood or heavy cardboard. Sift over the bottom a one-inch-deep layer of a mixture of one part dry, fine sand to two parts powdered borax. Place the individual flowers on this, not touching each other. Sift more of the mixture over the blooms, completely covering them. In five or six days, these flowers, still brightly colored, will be dry and ready for a season indoors.

Should you grow one or all of these separate gardens, or should you merely incorporate some of these flowers into your existing beds, you will find annuals most rewarding plants to grow.

FOUR GARDEN PLANS

*I Twelve Easy, Sturdy, Foolproof Annuals
in a Garden 12 by 4 Feet*

1. Baby's Breath (*Gypsophila elegans*) 2 ft.
2. Cockscomb, plumed (*Celosia argentea*) 15 in.
3. Dahlia, dwarf (*D. coccinea* and hybrids) 2½ ft.
4. Lobelia (*L. erinus speciosa*) 10 in.
5. Marigold (*Tagetes* varieties) 3 ft.
6. Phlox, annual dwarf (*P. drummondii*) 6 in.
7. Pincushion Flower (*Scabiosa atropurpurea*) 2 ft.
8. Stock (*Matthiola incana*) 15 in.
9. Tithonia (*T. rotundifolia*) 3 ft.
10. Verbena (*V. hortensis*) 12 in.
11. Zinnias, dwarf (*Z. angustifolia* varieties) 12 in.
12. Zinnias, tall (*Z. elegans* varieties) 3 ft.

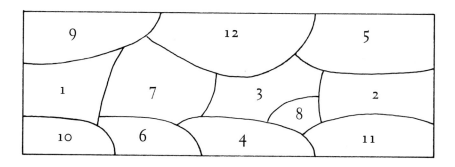

II Seven Vividly Colored Annuals
for a Corner Garden 6 by 6 Feet

1. Cockscomb (*Celosia argentea*), red, gold 15 in.
2. Flossflower (*Ageratum houstonianum*), blue 8 in.
3. Marigolds (*Tagetes* varieties), gold, yellow 3 ft.
4. Nasturtium, dwarf (*Tropaeolum majus* 'Tom Thumb'), orange, red shades 12 in.
5. Stock (*Matthiola incana*), white 15 in.
6. Zinnias, dwarf (*Z. angustifolia* varieties), all colors except blue 12 in.
7. Zinnias, tall (*Z. elegans* varieties), all colors except blue 3 ft.

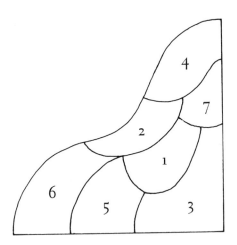

III Fifteen Unusual Annuals
in a Free-Form Border 15 Feet Long

1. African Daisy (*Arctotis stoechadifolia grandis*) 10 in.
2. Angel's Trumpet (*Datura metel*) 3 ft.
3. Baby Blue-Eyes (*Nemophila menziesii*) 9 in.
4. Black-Eyed-Susan Vine (*Thunbergia alata*) 1½ ft.
5. Butterfly Flower (*Schizanthus pinnatus*) 2½ ft.
6. Cupflower (*Nierembergia caerulea*) 6 in.
7. Love-in-a-Mist (*Nigella damascena*) 15 in.
8. Nemesia (*N. strumosa*) 12 in.
9. Phacelia (*P. campanularia*) 9 in.
10. Poppy-Mallow (*Callirhoe digitata*) 2½ ft.
11. Salpiglossis (*S. sinuata*) 2½ ft.
12. Star of Texas (*Xanthisma texanum*) 1½ ft.
13. Swan River Daisy (*Brachycome iberidifolia*) 12 in.
14. Salvia (*Salvia splendens*) 3 ft.
15. Bells-of-Ireland (*Molucella laevis*) 20 in.

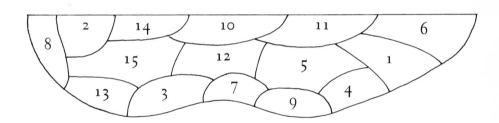

IV Annuals for Summer Beauty and Winter Bouquets in a Bed 12 by 4 Feet

1. Baby's Breath (*Gypsophila elegans*)
2. Bells-of-Ireland (*Molucella laevis*)
3. Cockscomb, plumed (*Celosia argentea plumosa*)
4. Globe Amaranth (*Gomphrena globosa*)
5. Honesty (*Lunaria annua*)
6. Immortelle (*Xeranthemum annuum*)
7. Job's Tears (*Coix lacryma-jobi*)
8. Statice (*Limonium sinuatum*)
9. Strawflower (*Helichrysum bracteatum*)
10. Sunray (*Helipterum roseum*)

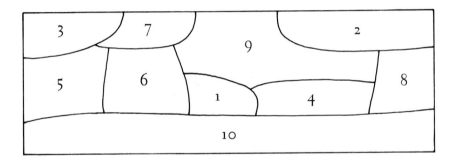

3. Marigolds
Give All You Can Ask

The Marigold is among the most satisfying and foolproof annuals. It offers appealing color and form, adaptability, a long bloom season, easy care. If you've never sown a seed in your life, don't let that stop you, for you literally can't keep a good Marigold down.

First of their many advantages is their great variety of color and size. Marigolds range through the warm, tawny shades, from pale yellow to deep orange and scarlet-mahogany. In 1975, the W. Atlee Burpee Company offered an exciting mixture of white and near-white semi-double blooms measuring up to three inches across. Mrs. Alice Vonk of Sully, Iowa, created this variety in 1975, winning the ten-thousand-dollar award offered by Burpee as long ago as 1954.

Some Marigold blooms are as large as five inches across, some as small as half an inch. The plants vary from six inches to four feet in height. Also, the tweedy-looking seeds germinate readily and rapidly, and the plants thrive in almost any soil. Undiscouraged by summer heat, they bloom continually through the season and up to the first heavy frost.

A favorite flower of the Aztecs and Incas, the Marigold originally came from the mountain slopes of Mexico and South America, where it still runs riot.

Full sun brings out the best in Marigolds. In semishade they run to foliage. In windy places they grow low and sturdy. At the seashore they develop extra-vivid tones, due perhaps to heavy dews and brilliant light. Sandy soil or light garden loam are preferred. Often these vigorous plants do beautifully in poor soil, but they will languish in heavy clay or very acid earth.

The fact that Marigolds don't start to bloom until late May or

June can be turned to advantage. When the foliage of perennials such as Oriental poppies and bleedinghearts disappears, Marigolds cheerfully fill the gap. Likewise, they can be used in beds of spring bulbs to screen the none too beautiful ripening greenery. And at the base of spring-flowering shrubs (on the south side) they will carry color on through the season.

You can, some May morning, decide you want a Marigold garden and by afternoon have one in full bloom. The origin of this miracle is the local nursery, where you can buy flats of Marigolds in flower ready to put right in the ground.

Wonderful results also come from raising your own Marigolds from seed. You may sow them in a coldframe, greenhouse or sunny window in late March or April—not sooner, lest seedlings grow leggy waiting for the ground outdoors to warm. Plant seeds in flats or seed pans. Be sure containers are clean, and sow seed about a quarter of an inch deep in a well-moistened rooting medium.

You can use sterile material such as expanded mica, clean sand or sphagnum moss; or you may prefer the standard mix of equal parts loam, sand and peat moss. In the former mix there is less chance of disease (if the containers are really clean); but plant food must be added. In the latter there is more available plant food. Either will work well.

After seeding, place in the shade and cover the container with newspaper to retain moisture. Lift this once a day to air the soil surface and help prevent damping-off disease, which kills seedlings.

After four days, remove the cover and bring the container to sunlight. When seedlings have at least two true leaves, you can transplant to the garden—after the last frost.

Seed may also be sown out-of-doors. If you merely toss seed into casually dug earth, some Marigolds will appear and flower. But if you fulfill their few special desires they grow dramatically.

Wait until the earth in the sun feels warm to touch. Dig the soil to a spade's depth. Remove roots and stones. Work the surface of the soil to make a good seedbed. Add peat to the surface if the soil needs more humus. Add sand if it seems too heavy.

Sow the seeds a quarter of an inch deep in a trench four inches wide, letting them fall about a half inch apart. Cover with soil, press firmly down. To hasten germination, water gently with a fine spray and cover with wet burlap. As with those indoors, after four days remove the cover. When seedlings have their true leaves, thin out the weakest ones and transplant extras to wherever you desire. Soak the soil before and after the move. Place the tall varieties eight to ten inches apart, the low ones six to eight inches. This may seem close, as each tall variety, if allowed to, will broaden to two feet, and the low ones to one foot. But close planting makes a solid show of color and allows for any casualties.

Cultural requirements for keeping Marigolds healthy are simple and few. For abundant and continuous bloom make it a habit to pick flowers for bouquets, and cut off dead flower heads of the larger sorts. Marigold roots are near the surface, so cultivate gently around the stalk. It is good to summer-mulch with two to four inches of buckwheat hulls, rough compost or peat moss to hold moisture and deter weeds.

For many years there were but two distinct types of Marigold: the tall, large-flowered so-called "African" and the much smaller and more varied "French" Marigold, blooming on into November and providing long-lasting bouquets and fascinating garden effects with scarlet salvia and cannas. Today there are many more strains and horticultural developments from both types.

Whether you incorporate Marigolds into your perennial border or bed of mixed annuals or whether you grow them by themselves, they are among the most rewarding of all annuals.

4. Annuals That Come Again

The great thing about annuals is their fast growth, easy care and generous display of bloom. If they have a shortcoming, it is their brief life. A plant blooms for a season and is gone forever. But this cycle of growth, for which they are named, is not so limiting as it sounds.

We have discovered that many kinds of lovely annuals will reseed themselves and come up year after year. They do this so dependably that we almost think of them as "perennials."

These obliging flowers come in a wide range of colors, almost every shade, and a broad variety of shapes and sizes. Some of the flowers start to bloom in early spring and continue even through a frost or two. They are strong, hardy, easy to establish, tolerant of many kinds of soil and reasonably resistant to pests and diseases. What more can you ask of any flower?

To do their best, these amiable recurring annuals need a very minimum of five hours of sun a day, and the more the better. Grow them in any ordinary garden loam (on the sandy side preferred). In a seashore location colors will be unusually vivid. In a windy spot the plants will grow lower, with sturdier, thicker stems.

In the early spring the sun-warmed earth is ready for seed. The sooner these annuals go in, the sooner they will come up and flower. So lose not a moment in getting started. First spread a good fertilizer on the area you have chosen. We use a two- to four-inch layer of compost and barnyard manure. If, in your vicinity, the latter is difficult to obtain, any balanced commercial fertilizer will suffice. Turn this all over to a depth of six or eight inches, rake smooth, and let settle for a few days.

We sow short, curving, random rows, like arched eyebrows, all through the bed. This gives us a massed effect when the plants flower. We group two or three related colors and sizes together in drifts. Each "eyebrow," which might be anywhere from one to three feet long, is slightly depressed to catch the rain. We scatter seed in the shallow curving row, sprinkle soil lightly on top until each kind is covered to a depth of about twice its diameter, and then we press the soil down firmly. Plastic labels (we use plastic because the names erase and the labels may be used over again) mark each variety to show what is what. These definite curving rows enable you to distinguish the seedlings from surrounding weeds as both first appear. The labels help you to learn what each variety looks like.

In one to three weeks, depending on weather, twin leaves of the annuals push up into the sunlight, and the excitement begins.

And in these first few weeks of growth you get to know these tiny plants; each has quite a different character from its neighbor. Cosmos is feathery, even as a two-inch infant. Chinese Forget-Me-Not is furry. Nicotiana leaves lie flat, hugging the earth and looking like pale green confetti. You learn to tell one from the other as you live with them and watch them grow to two inches, three inches—until it's time to thin.

The first thinning should be done a month or six weeks after seeding. We like to let the plants develop not only their true leaves, but a few more. If you grow them somewhat beyond the first true-leaf stage, recommended by some, their hold on life will be even stronger.

As we do it, the thinning process is really transplanting, not pulling out and tossing away. We gently move the plants about, setting them here and there to fill in blank spaces. It's best to pick a misty day or late afternoon after a shower, when the soil is damp. Use a trowel to lift clusters of young plants, and then carefully separate them. Note, as you work with them, how they differ from weeds.

We thin most plants to stand about six inches apart, except the really tall ones, such as Cosmos and Spiderflower. These are thinned to one foot apart. This is somewhat closer than the books advise, but we like a compact mass of flowers. When plants are close together they shade out many weeds.

The transplanting process is a challenge. The less the seedlings wilt when moved, the sooner you will have flowers. It's best to pour a little water in each hole as you set the tiny plants. Then, when you firm the soil up around their necks, you have planted not only the seedlings but a small reservoir in which the newly growing roots establish themselves. After transplanting, soak again thoroughly, spray the earth and tops, and water daily until new growth starts. If the sun is hot, shade the smaller groupings with bushel baskets, the larger ones with cheese-cloth tied on garden stakes. It is worth this little extra effort to get these plants growing properly the first year, because this time is the last you will need to plant.

The needs of a "perennial garden of annuals" are few and simple. It wants to be free of weeds, and watered in a drought. A mulch of cocoa hulls, buckwheat hulls or grass clippings all but eliminates the need to weed or water. If a feeling of "tender loving care" comes over you, give them all some plant food in early summer (a few weeks after transplanting) and in August.

In autumn, when the pods are dry, pull up the flower stalks and shake out any remaining seeds. But by this time most of them will have already spread abroad by themselves. The stalks may be dropped where they stood and covered with a light mulch of hay or grass clippings to maintain a neat look.

In the spring remove these old stalks. There will be so many seeds in the area that if some get pushed underground, trampled on or blown away, no matter. Plenty will still come up. However, don't weed or disturb the ground until late spring, after the new seedlings are up and recognizable. By then the mulch will be disintegrating, adding nutriment to the soil, and keeping the ground soft.

To thin second-year seedlings, loosen the earth with a trowel. This much turning over is all that is needed. Incidentally, the arrangement and pattern this second year will be different from the first, depending on where the seeds happen to have dropped.

Here are the annuals that have come up year after year for us.

ALYSSUM *(Lobularia)* will reward you all summer not only with great sheets of flowers, but with a fine scent like that of new-mown hay.

CORNFLOWER *(Centaurea cyanus)*. These sprout, push up their gray-green foliage early and thrive despite temperamental weather. All the colors and varieties, especially the rich blue 'Jubilee Gem,' reward you aplenty. If you feel like giving them tender loving care, pick off the dead flower heads during the first part of summer. This extends the blooming period far into autumn. The related Sweet Sultan *(C. moschata)* bears two-inch-wide, densely double, fringed and fluffy flowers in white, lavender, rose-pink, or purple.

LARKSPUR *(Delphinium ajacis)* may go in early. It blooms from the beginning of summer to late frost, bringing every color except yellow to the garden. The deep, dark, electric blue variety is one of the most dramatic. Larkspur is an annual Delphinium.

And now wait a bit until the oak leaves grow to the size of a mouse's ear; then plant the other annuals.

PETUNIA *(P. hybrida)* flowers from early June to late fall the second and following years. The first year the blooms begin in July. The second year they may not reappear in the colors originally sown, but seeing what does come is part of the fun. And once you have Petunias, you always have Petunias.

PORTULACA *(P. grandiflora)* is a remarkably indomitable plant. It reappears another season not only in the garden where it is supposed to grow, but it also flings its giddy colors over our gravel drive, cropping up between rocks and stones. The fleshy foliage holds water, and the driest of locations or seasons doesn't discourage it.

WISHBONE FLOWER *(Torenia fournieri).* In the heart of each deep violet-blue flower lies a small, delicate white "wishbone." This is a glowing, cheery little border plant.

DWARF MARIGOLD *(Tagetes).* The single and double French and pygmy types, especially *Tagetes pumila,* will come again in a gratifying manner. They are sunny, gay flowers, with a background of Mexican lore. Years ago, the Aztec priests used to mingle dried Marigold flowers with dried tobacco and, inhaling the smoke, induce a trance. We have resisted the urge to try this.

SNAPDRAGON *(Antirrhinum majus).* These well-loved blooms come in every color but blue. Their fine seeds need special care. Work the seedbed to a smooth, even texture. Scatter the seeds and mingle them with the soil surface. Cover the area lightly with fine soil and press down. Snapdragon seed is slow to germinate (three weeks, at least), and, for the first year, slow to flower. In the following years it will flower earlier.

SUMMER FORGET-ME-NOT *(Anchusa capensis)* is one of two fine blues. The bushy, erect plants are well covered with sprays of blossoms like true Forget-Me-Nots, each with a white eye. I've never known a bug or any other wildlife to disturb *Anchusa's* stiff, hairy foliage or flowers.

CHINESE FORGET-ME-NOT *(Cynoglossum amabile)* has indigo-blue blossoms, and, be it ever so hot and dry, this plant thrives all summer.

Look at the tiny florets through a magnifying glass—they are exquisite.

POT MARIGOLD (*Calendula officinalis*) and GAILLARDIA (*G. pulchella* hybrids) are distant cousins that bring the giddy colors of Mexico to the garden. Pot Marigolds (also called Calendulas) are zinnia-like flowers in tones of apricot, pale yellow, deep yellow, and persimmon-orange. They are a grand cut flower for indoors, sturdy and long-lasting.

As to Gaillardias, not only are all the hues of Mexico caught in their tones, but all of autumn, and sunset colors everywhere. They come single and double; some blossoms are three inches across with smoky red quills or gold-tipped quills, some are in other wonderful color combinations.

FLOWERING TOBACCO or NICOTIANA (*Nicotiana alata*) is the annual with perhaps the greatest zest for living. Once you adopt it you never lose it, and you never want to, for its white starry flowers emit their tropical scent morning and night when they spangle your garden. At noon, in the heat of summer, the flowers droop, creating, strangely enough, a pleasant pattern in which the broad flat leaves stand out and attract attention. In the cool of afternoon the flowers perk up, and at dusk they greet your dinner guests with their purity and fragrance. Nicotiana keeps on blooming best if cut back or completely picked in late July and September.

SPIDERFLOWER (*Cleome spinosa*) is a special favorite of ours. Naturalized from the West Indies, it grows wild in both brilliant sun and semishade along the roadsides in southern Connecticut and Rhode Island. It will return every season to your garden where you have planted it and, mysteriously, where you have not. The trusses of salmon-pink flowers, thinly settled atop the stalk, bloom from summer to fall.

COSMOS (*C. bipinnatus*), with its yellow-centered daisylike flowers, graces any bed of annuals. The colors are lavender, orange, pink, yellow, and white, and the wide petals have a charming deckled edge.

I am sure there are a great many other annuals besides these that will reseed. I have included here only those with which we have had direct experience. Each year we try a few new varieties. We never tire of this garden because it is never the same. The blossoms that are featured one year may play a supporting role the following summer while something else dominates the scene. The suspense, the surprise, and their easygoing character place these "perennial" annuals in a class by themselves.

Part Two

ONE HUNDRED PERENNIALS

5. One Hundred Perennials

FLOWERS THAT START IN SPRING

DAPHNE (*D. genkwa*). Mezereum ▶
Family
Out of Korea and Japan comes this
rare and delightful plant, actually a
small deciduous shrub. The stunning
light blue or lavender flowers are borne
in clusters along last year's branches,
and open very early, well ahead of the
foliage. Branches may be cut in late
winter and forced indoors for surprise
blooms while snow covers the ground
outdoors. The fruits are white berries.
> HEIGHT: 3 feet.
> COLOR: Lilac-blue.
> LOCATION: Warm and sunny
spot.
> SOIL: Well-drained garden loam,
moderately acid.
> PROPAGATION: Start from seed.
> USES: Ideal in the flower border
in front of a shrub border.
> FRAGRANT. Subtle scent.
> CULTURAL HINTS: Not for the
colder parts of the country because it
needs a long summer ripening. Protect
with straw in winter. Water sparingly
in summer.

PASQUEFLOWER (*Anemone
pulsatilla*). Buttercup Family
Fur-covered early-spring foliage protects
this lovely and graceful plant from late
freezes. The rich violet blooms with
gold centers open when robins return in
spring. The seedpods, a tangled mass
of silken hairs, are as appealing as the
flowers. Flourishes in the wild on

▲

chalky downs in Great Britain and
parts of Europe, especially the Swiss
Alps.
> HEIGHT: 9 to 12 inches.
> COLOR: Violet (recent varieties
also in white and rose).
> LOCATION: Cool, moist location
in the rock garden. Sun or partial
shade.
> SOIL: Rich, limy garden loam.
Must be well drained.
> PROPAGATION: Set out plants six
to eight inches apart in spring or fall.
Make root divisions in early spring.
Also start from seed.
> USES: In front of the border; in
the rock garden; does best in a moraine.
> CULTURAL HINTS: Give lime once
or twice during the summer. Sifted
wood ashes are very beneficial when
scattered on the ground around the
plants.

▲

LUNGWORT; BLUE COWSLIP
(*Pulmonaria angustifolia*).
Borage Family
In early May, forget-me-not-colored flowers cover the plant, making it a good companion to spring bulbs. It is tough and hardy, and multiplies readily. The botanical name is derived from the Latin *Pulmo*, meaning "lung," because of a belief in the efficacy of the leaves in treating lung troubles.

HEIGHT: 8 to 10 inches.

COLOR: Sky blue (i.e., the form *azurea*), but there are deeper blue, white, and even red varieties.

LOCATION: A cool, partly shaded position. Sometimes does well in full sun.

SOIL: Heavy, moist soil, but well drained.

PROPAGATION: Plant ten inches apart. Root division in early spring or fall. Water thoroughly after separating. Also grows well from seed; will bloom the following year.

USES: Rock gardens; the front of the flower border.

CULTURAL HINTS: Incorporate peat moss, compost or leafmold into the soil once a year. Divide clumps every third year for abundant bloom.

CREEPING PHLOX; MOSS-PINK
(*P. subulata*). Phlox Family
An indestructible plant with mosslike evergreen foliage. Splendid for the rockery or for hot dry banks where you want year-round groundcover. No weeds can penetrate this heavy matted greenery. Early in the spring, masses of

▲

flowers completely hide the tiny leaves with drifts of cheery color. A native of eastern North America, this plant grows wild from New York to North Carolina and Kentucky.

HEIGHT: 6 inches.

COLOR: Pink, white, blue, violet, crimson (also a violent magenta that may be well to avoid, at least in quantity).

LOCATION: Full sun. Open, well-drained position.

SOIL: Well-drained soil, light and porous. Loam that is slightly gritty.

PROPAGATION: Set plants eight to twelve inches apart. Divide clumps after blooming and cut back the tops of the new transplants.

USES: Rock gardens; banks; among rocks at the top of a stone wall.

FRAGRANT. Meadowy scent in the sun.

CULTURAL HINTS: Allow plenty of room for spreading. Cultivate frequently to keep soil loose and friable.

▲

ROCK CRESS (*Arabis alpina*).
Mustard Family
Originally from Arabia, hence the
botanical name *Arabis*. Also found in
protected passes and high valleys in the
Swiss mountains. Flourishes in the
chinks of walls, rock gardens, flower
borders. Sheets of flowers spread over
silvery-gray foliage soon after the last
snows. The delightful fresh fragrance
seeks you out in other parts of the
garden.
> HEIGHT: 6 inches.
> COLOR: White.
> LOCATION: Sun or partial shade.
> SOIL: Sandy soil and good
drainage.
> PROPAGATION: Seeds. Root divi-
sions also, but take these soon after
flowering, and set six inches apart.
> USES: Fine for the front of the
border. All edging. Let tumble over
rock walls, steep banks. Good cut
flowers for a small vase.
> FRAGRANT. A fresh, cool fra-
grance.
> CULTURAL HINTS: Give frequent
feedings of bone meal or well-rotted
manure. Keep on the dry side. Cut the
plants back after flowering to produce
new growth and keep compact.

SWEET VIOLET; FLORIST'S
VIOLET (*Viola odorata*). Violet
Family
Eat the flowers candied and the young
leaves in salads. Thrives in Southern
gardens and indoors in a greenhouse in
the North. A cheerful, well-loved
flower, delightful to pick for small
bouquets and corsages. Keeps on blooming for a long season. A favorite of
Napoleon, who always presented
Josephine with a bouquet of Sweet
Violets on the anniversary of their
wedding. Used in medicine since the
time of the Greeks. Syrup of Violets
was considered to be of value for
children long years ago.
> HEIGHT: 4 to 6 inches.
> COLOR: Violet, white, old rose,
clear blue.
> LOCATION: Half sun.
> SOIL: Rich, well-drained soil with
plenty of organic matter, compost and
leafmold.
> PROPAGATION: By seed and root
division. Very easy to propagate, as it
sends out runners. Plants grow strongly
and may be divided every year or so.
Set eight inches apart.
> USES: Wonderful in the rock
garden or border. Fits well into the
wild garden or a woodland area. Hanging baskets on the porch, where you
will enjoy the fragrance.
> FRAGRANT. Deep and penetrating
scent.
> CULTURAL HINTS: Should be kept
damp at all times. Keep faded flowers
picked off to encourage continuous
bloom. Feed frequently with a balanced
plant food. Give a mulch of hay or
straw in winter.

ALYSSUM; BASKET OF GOLD (A. *saxatile citrinum*). Mustard Family
Clusters of honey-sweet pale gold flowers nearly hide the gray foliage in April and May. Tumbles over rocks. The soft yellow brings sunshine to the garden, even in rain. (The type form, A. *saxatile*, is often too intense and overwhelming in color.) One of the most popular perennials for the garden, it is a sturdy, dependable, profuse bloomer. The plant was said to calm the unbalanced mind. The Greek word *alyssum* means "to allay rage." Blooms to some extent throughout the summer.
HEIGHT: To 8 inches.
COLOR: Lemon-yellow.
LOCATION: Full sun.
SOIL: Average garden loam, preferably slightly acid to neutral, with good drainage.
PROPAGATION: Seed, divisions. Set plants ten inches apart.

USES: In rock gardens, along rock walls. Fine for edging, bordering walks, hanging baskets, or window boxes.
FRAGRANT. Honey-sweet fragrant flowers.
CULTURAL HINTS: Alyssum must have a full-sun location. Keep on the dry side and feed occasionally to stimulate growth. Must have well-drained soil; add sand and grit if necessary. Cut back after flowering, and keep new plants coming on, for it is not too long-lived.

◄ BUNCH PRIMROSE (*Primula polyantha*). Primrose Family
This is a group of hybrids of garden origin, but its parentage is uncertain—usually thought to be P. *vulgaris* and P. *officinalis*. Among the most colorful, varied and easily grown of hundreds of kinds of primroses, and a favorite of English gardeners for generations. Disraeli was particularly fond of it. Each plant in full flower is like a nosegay and lasts a long time in bloom. The botanical name (*Primula*) derives from the Latin *primus*, meaning "first," and refers to the early bloom (May).
HEIGHT: 5-to-10-inch flower stems to the wrinkled leaves at the base of the plant.
COLOR: Yellow, apricot, blue, red, rose, white.
LOCATION: Part shade or full shade.
SOIL: Rich, moist loam, well drained, with ample humus.
PROPAGATION: By plant division or seed. Set plants eight inches apart.
USES: Every perennial border needs Primroses. Popular in rockeries; also in naturalized woodlands, where you might scatter them or walk a Primrose path. In bog gardens—not in the water, but near it.
FRAGRANT. Subtle scent.
CULTURAL HINTS: Divide the plants every few years. Must be kept moist at all times. Will not survive a summer drought. In cultivating, be careful not to disturb the roots. Mulch in winter.

PERIWINKLE; RUNNING-
MYRTLE *(Vinca minor)*. Dogbane
Family
Solid mass of glossy evergreen leaves
starred with white or blue flowers.
Ideal ground cover under trees. Grows
wild in Britain. Possibly introduced by
the Romans, who wove the green
streamers of leaves into wreaths for
special ceremonial occasions. In the
fourteenth century it was called by the
glamorous name of "Joy of the
Ground." In the language of flowers, it
is the "pleasures of memory." The
botanical name *Vinca* comes from the
Latin *vinculum*, meaning "a band,"
and refers to the long, supple stems.

HEIGHT: To 6 inches.
COLOR: White, blue.
LOCATION: Shade and part sun.
SOIL: Average garden loam.
PROPAGATION: Root division. Set
new plants four to six inches apart.
The running shoots root as they grow.
New plants are readily produced on
the runners.
USES: As edging to shrubbery
borders. A beautiful carpet to cover the
ground under trees. To grow in areas
where bulbs are planted. A ground
cover for a fern bed.
CULTURAL HINTS: Thin every few
years.

COLUMBINE *(Aquilegia)*. Buttercup
Family
The botanical name comes from the
Latin *aquila*, meaning eagle, and refers
to the deeply spurred petals. These
light, swinging blossoms enhance the
spot they grow in and are favorites of
almost everyone. The species *A. caerulea* is the state flower of Colorado.
After the flowers fade, the foliage,
somewhat suggestive of the maidenhair
fern, beautifies the garden the rest of
the summer, and even into autumn.
The leaves acquire interesting and
subtle tints to compete with fall colors
of other plants. A perfect perennial.

HEIGHT: 6 to 30 inches, differing
among individuals as well as varieties.
COLOR: Blue, lavender, yellow,
pink, white, red, according to various
species and hybrids.
LOCATION: Full sun, part shade.
Sheltered spot.
SOIL: Rich, light garden loam,
well drained.
PROPAGATION: Easily raised from
seed. Flowers the second season and
one or two seasons thereafter, but is
not long-lived and should be replaced
by new seedlings. Set plants ten inches
apart.
USES: Important flowers for the
perennial border, where they tend to
steal the show with their long, trailing
spurs and delicate colors and form.
Fine as cut flowers.
CULTURAL HINTS: For added
vigor give feedings of leafmold during
the summer. The plants need protection from the wind, as the stems are
delicate. Mulch for winter protection.

BLEEDINGHEART (*Dicentra* ▶
spectabilis). Fumitory Family
A native of China. If you take a blossom apart you find in its center a perfect miniature harp, a rabbit, and a bottle! After the blooms fade the beautiful blue-green foliage dies and disappears. But do not be alarmed. The plant is not dead. The feathery fernlike leaves return the following spring. In the meantime, their place could be filled with some shallow-rooted annuals in bloom.

HEIGHT: 12 to 24 inches.
COLOR: Pink, white.
LOCATION: Partial shade, cool location. Does not do well where summers are long and hot.
SOIL: Rich garden loam.
PROPAGATION: Division of plants in the early, early spring, or when the foliage dies down in midsummer.
USES: Fine plants to set in shaded areas in front of shrubs and for the perennial border.
CULTURAL HINTS: Keep the plants moist all season. Never let them become bone dry. Stake if your location is windy. Feed with rotted manure in the spring and cultivate the ground frequently.

▲

the early fall and set one foot apart.
USES: A fine edging plant. Good in the rockery or the front of the perennial border. Appropriate for hanging baskets and porch boxes.
CULTURAL HINTS: Keep well watered and feed regularly.

CANDYTUFT (*Iberis sempervirens*).
Mustard Family
The botanical name comes from Iberia (Spain), where the original species abounds. Also native to Persia. A plant attractive not only in spring bloom but throughout the summer, with its rich, green foliage. For weeks in the spring the foliage remains all but hidden beneath masses of showy white flowers in clusters. It is impervious to the vagaries of weather; therefore, in the language of flowers, this one stands for indifference.

HEIGHT: To 1 foot.
COLOR: White.
LOCATION: Full sun.
SOIL: Rich soil, well drained, but will endure dry ground.
PROPAGATION: By seed sown in the spring. Plants may be divided in

GERMAN or TALL BEARDED IRIS
(*I. germanica*). Iris Family
An easy-to-grow plant, fine for beginners. The genus is one of the oldest of garden plants. One kind, brought from Syria to Egypt by Thutmos in 1501 B.C., is found in a bas-relief in his temple at Karnak. A fifth-century king, Clovis, observed the Iris growing in a river and realized the stream was shallow enough to ford. Thus he saved his army. In gratitude, he adopted the Iris as his emblem. This symbol was long used. The Iris is believed to be the origin of the Fleur-de-lis.

HEIGHT: 1 to 3 feet.
COLOR: Every color.
LOCATION: Sunny location.
SOIL: Well-drained, light soil, preferably alkaline.
PROPAGATION: Division of rhizomes. Should be divided in August,

▲

every three years. Also grows readily from seed.

Uses: Adapts well to the perennial border. Dwarf types are excellent in a rock garden or for edging.

Fragrant. Subtle sweet scent.

Cultural hints: Feed a balanced food for best results. Iris appreciate wood ashes in the soil. Cultivate very carefully, if at all, as the rhizomes are near the surface and like to bake in the midsummer sun.

BUGLE FLOWER; BUGLEWEED
(*Ajuga genevensis*). Mint Family
Low spikes of small two-lipped florets in whorls around leafy stems, make a mist of blue for many weeks in May and June. This is a plant you can't keep down. It carpets the ground so thickly, hardly a weed can get through. A superb ground cover for difficult banks, shady stretches under trees, places where not much else will grow. The foliage develops a bronze-purple metallic sheen in fall and winter. Evergreen most of the year in a mild climate.

Height: 6 to 9 inches.

Color: Blue.

Location: Sun, shade. Adapts to all locations.

Soil: Average soil. Adjusts to most kinds of earth.

Propagation: Divides successfully all summer long. Any time after a rain, plants may be separated and moved.

Uses: Fine as a ground cover under trees and in rockgardens. Good for edging.

Cultural hints: Keep within bounds by pulling up or trimming back the plants that spread beyond where you want them to grow. A fine plant to share with friends. ◄

BLUE PHLOX; WILD SWEET WILLIAM (*P. divaricata canadensis*). Phlox Family
Thrives in drifts under trees. A member of a vast and almost entirely North American family. Useful in the garden in borders, rock gardens, wooded slopes, thin woodland. Easy to grow, popular, and beloved by children and beginners as well as more sophisticated gardeners. The florets are borne in graceful loose clusters and cover the plant entirely in May.

Height: To 15 inches.

Color: Lavender-blue.

Location: Part shade.

Soil: Light loam.

Propagation: Divide roots in the spring. Set six inches apart.

Uses: Good in places where later bloom or foliage will quickly conceal its shabby look right after flowering. For that reason, it is not really a good edging plant.

Fragrant. Nice meadowy fragrance.

Cultural hints: Feed at intervals during the summer and mulch in winter in a cold climate.

▼

SNOW-IN-SUMMER (*Cerastium tomentosum*). Pink Family
Masses of snowy flowers spill over silvery-white foliage. Trails down banks and over rocks, creating a cascade of bloom. Thrives and spreads even in soil that is almost pure sand. The botanical name *Cerastium* comes from the Greek *kerastes*, horned, and refers to the form of the pod. A popular flower some of which everyone should grow somewhere. Wonderfully cool-looking in hot weather.
◄ looking in hot weather.

HEIGHT: 6 to 8 inches.
COLOR: White.
LOCATION: Full sun, dry location.
SOIL: Average.
PROPAGATION: From seed and division of roots. Set young plants in the shade until they have developed good root systems of their own.
USES: A rock-garden favorite, as it spreads gracefully over the boulders For use on banks, if kept under control, and superb in dry stone walls. Also a good edging plant for walks and borders.
CULTURAL HINTS: Give a liberal amount of food in the early spring.

◄ORIENTAL POPPY (*Papaver orientale*). Poppy Family
One of the most beautiful and dramatic of all perennials. Nothing is more spectacular than the tissue-paper-like petals of the great blooms when they have just unfolded. The flower center is dark—sometimes black—and the flower parts, anthers and stamens, tremble in the slightest zephyr. To use as cut flowers pick blooms just opened and dip the stems briefly in boiling water. This helps them to last several days. Ceres is usually represented as wearing a garland of mingled grain and Poppies. It was believed that growing Poppies in the grainfields benefited the grain.

HEIGHT: 2 to 3 feet.
COLOR: Scarlet, pink, white.
LOCATION: Full sun—and make

sure to plant the long taproot deep, its top about three inches below the soil surface.

SOIL: Rich garden loam, well drained and light, with plenty of humus.

PROPAGATION: To multiply Poppies, pot up separately a few four-inch slices of the root. Also may be grown from seed. Set young plants ten inches apart.

USES: In the perennial border. Massed in front of shrubbery. Beautiful when planted with lupine and bearded iris—all will be in bloom at once. Very exciting.

CULTURAL HINTS: Feed the plants regularly with a balanced fertilizer. Cover with well-rotted manure in fall for winter protection. Water during the flowering season. Once established, do not move.

ANCHUSA *(Brunnera macrophylla)*.
Borage Family
A misty sea of blue flowers against silvery-mottled foliage. Self-sows in places where the parent plants grow well. The plant was formerly called *Anchusa myosotideflora. Anchusa*, in Greek, means "a dye." Dye and rouge were made from the roots long years ago by the ancients. Now properly rechristened *Brunnera macrophylla*, from its large and lush summer leaves. A native of the Caucasus and Siberia.

HEIGHT: 6 to 12 inches.

COLOR: Blue.

LOCATION: Full sun, half sun.

SOIL: Good rich soil.

PROPAGATION: Division of plants in very early spring. Also sow seed for flowering the second season.

USES: In the front of the border, rock gardens.

CULTURAL HINTS: Feed periodically with a balanced fertilizer, and in the spring give well-rotted manure and bone meal. Never let the plants become dry. Trim off faded flowers and the plants will have a second blooming. ▶

THYME *(Thymus vulgaris)*.
Mint Family
Thrives in a soil rich in lime. Flourishes among rocks and is impervious to drought. The Swiss country people say to boil Thyme in milk and drink the mixture to cure a cough. It has been used for many years as a seasoning for a variety of foods. Native to the Mediterranean region, where it grows wild, covering the hillsides and filling the air with a pungent scent. It is also found in many other places from Iceland to the Himalayas. Symbol of energy and activity. A fine honey comes from Mount Hymettus, a mountain carpeted with wild thyme, in Greece. The plant is a great favorite of bees.

HEIGHT: 3 to 6 inches.

COLOR: Pink, lavender, in May and June.

LOCATION: Sun.

SOIL: Well-drained, sandy soil, not too rich. Prefers alkaline soil.

PROPAGATION: Division and seed.

USES: In rock gardens. Between stepping stones in a path. Bordering terraces. In cooking, a popular seasoning.

FRAGRANT. The foliage has a deep, penetrating scent when crushed in the fingers or stepped on.

CULTURAL HINTS: Put wood ashes around the plants in the spring.

AUBRIETIA; AUBRETIA; PURPLE
ROCK CRESS (*Aubrietia deltoidea*).
Mustard Family
Native from Sicily to Asia Minor.
Cushions of triangular silvery-green
hairy leaves blanketed with flowers.
Thrives between random flagging.
Named for Claude Aubriet, a French
painter of natural history subjects of
the nineteenth century.
HEIGHT: 3 to 6 inches.
COLOR: Purple; but also lavender,
white, and dark red-violet.
LOCATION: Partial sun; dry,
cool area.
SOIL: Light, sandy, well-drained
soil.
PROPAGATION: Division of the
mats or clumps.
USES: Perennial bed, border or
rockery, wherever you desire. A spreading plant. Fine for edging.
CULTURAL HINTS: Feed occasionally with a balanced plant food. Keep
on the dry side. Does not do well
where summers are long and hot. Does
do well in England.

SEA-PINK; THRIFT (*Armeria
maritima*). Plumbago Family
Blooms in hot, dry areas, especially at
the seashore. Flowers spring up among
tangled grasslike leaves. Native to
Europe, West Asia, North Africa and
North America. Also grows in Iceland.
Sometimes erroneously called Statice.
HEIGHT: 10 to 12 inches.
COLOR: White, pink, purple.
LOCATION: Full sun and dry area.

SOIL: Light, sandy loam with
good drainage. It likes chalky soil when
growing near the sea, but there are
alpine forms found on granite.
PROPAGATION: Division of root
systems. Also seed.
USES: A fine edging plant along
driveways, paths or borders. Excellent
in the rock garden.
CULTURAL HINTS: Cover in
winter with a mulch of leaves and
branches. Feed occasionally with a
balanced fertilizer.

TRUE PANSY (*Viola wittrockiana*).
Violet Family
Gayest of all spring flowers. Perky and
smiling. Sometimes the same plant
lives for years, but in general best
treated as a biennial. Blooms almost
all summer, slowing up during hot and
dry spells, then getting a second wind
and continuing until frost. The lines

▼

on the lower petals guide visiting insects to the heart of the plant for nectar.

HEIGHT: 8 inches.
COLOR: All colors.
LOCATION: Part sun.
SOIL: Rich, well-drained soil, with ample organic matter.
PROPAGATION: Seed. Or buy and set out young plants.
USES: Fine for edging, borders, rock gardens. Perfect for hanging baskets, porch boxes, window boxes.
FRAGRANT. A lovely soft scent.
CULTURAL HINTS: Keep the fading blossoms picked off for a long period of bloom. Keep watered during a dry spell. Best to have the soil damp most of the time.

GARLAND FLOWER (*Daphne cneorum*). Mezereum Family
The small light-green finger-shaped leaves are evergreen. Grows wild in the mountain meadows of Switzerland and southern Europe, trailing over boulders at the high passes. Fragrant dried flowers scent the linen closet. Will take temperatures to 10 degrees below zero. Cover with leaves and branches in winter.

HEIGHT: 8 inches.
COLOR: Pink.
LOCATION: Full sun.
SOIL: Light, well-drained soil. Loam, leafmold and limestone in equal parts. Roots in the shade, foliage in the sun is ideal.
PROPAGATION: Seed.

▼

USES: Excellent in the perennial border. Grows well in the rockery with other shrubs. Flowers make lovely bouquets.
FRAGRANT. Deeply scented.
CULTURAL HINTS: Keep moist during the spring and summer months. In the North, cover the plant with a piece of burlap until all danger of frost is over.

PERENNIAL FLAX (*Linum perenne*). Flax Family
The flowers of this plant open only in early sunshine and close by noon. Various species are among the oldest plants known to man. Relics have been found in prehistoric dwellings dating back before even the use of cereals was known. The Egyptians wrapped their mummies in cloth made from flax. Before cotton was developed, Flax was widely used for making clothes. To see a farmer sowing a field of this plant prompted the remark that he was sowing his own shirts. It is much culti-. vated in southern Germany today.

HEIGHT: 18 inches.
COLOR: Chicory blue, white.
LOCATION: Full sun and airy spot.
SOIL: Average soil, well drained.
PROPAGATION: Seed.
USES: A charming and unusual border plant. Grows well with larkspur, lupine, delphinium.
CULTURAL HINTS: Cultivate during the summer. Keep fairly moist at all times. When flowering is over, cut back to six inches. ▼

FORGET-ME-NOT (*Myosotis scorpioides*). Borage Family
They say, "Wear these and your love will never forget you." These are the old-fashioned Forget-Me-Nots, blue and pink. Enchanting in tiny bouquets and corsages. Delightful thriving along a stream, where they will spread and eventually border the brook for many yards. They bloom for weeks. A northern plant, across much of Siberia, and from Lapland to Madeira.

HEIGHT: 6 inches.
COLOR: Blue, sometimes pink, with yellow, pink, or white eye.
LOCATION: Part sun. Flourishes with the roots in running water.
SOIL: Rich, dark soil with plenty of organic matter.
PROPAGATION: Seed and plant division.
USES: Fine in the border, or for underplanting in the rock garden. Also in hanging baskets and in the wild garden.
FRAGRANT. Cool and fresh fragrance.
CULTURAL HINTS: Keep moist at all times. Feed a balanced plant food regularly. Mulch in winter with dry leaves.

PROPAGATION: Seed and division.
USES: Fine for a border, for rock gardens, for edging, porch boxes, hanging baskets.
FRAGRANT. Mildly fragrant.
CULTURAL HINTS: Keep moist at all times. Feed with balanced food several times during the summer. Remove fading flowers for longer, heavier blooming.

TUFTED VIOLA; PANSY; HORNED VIOLET (*V. cornuta*). Violet Family
Introduced from the Pyrenees in 1776. Used by the ton for perfume in Syria and Turkey; also in preparation of a national drink, a kind of sherbet. This solid-color pansy with a gold center blooms from the last snows of winter until the first snows of the next. Perennial in moderately mild regions, elsewhere a biennial, blooming in June from seed sown indoors in March. Several fine named hybrids.
HEIGHT: 8 inches.
COLOR: Blue, purple, apricot, yellow.
LOCATION: Semishade and full sun.
SOIL: Rich, well-drained soil, with ample organic matter.

JOHNNY-JUMP-UP; WILD PANSY (*Viola tricolor*). Violet Family
In Elizabethan times this plant was called Heart's Ease. Reseeds where it grows; scatters across the garden. Blooms intermittently all winter if the climate is somewhat mild. A charming, perky little plant, its small two- or three-colored flowers are utterly bewitching in tiny bouquets and small homemade corsages. Wear a few in your hair, your buttonhole, and pick them for the house.
HEIGHT: 6 inches.
COLOR: Yellow, maroon, blue.
LOCATION: Full sun.
SOIL: Rich, well-drained soil, with plenty of organic matter.
PROPAGATION: Seed, division.
USES: Fine for the border, for rock gardens, for edging, porch boxes, hanging baskets.

FRAGRANT. Delightfully aromatic.

CULTURAL HINTS: Trim the plant back during the summer twice to induce ample blooms. Keep moist at all times. Feed often during the summer.

◀ GEUM (*G. chiloense*). Rose Family
A native of Chile, where it carpets the mountainsides and is as brilliant as the native costumes. Only recently introduced into cultivation. The name comes from the Greek, *geuo*, meaning " a fine flavor," in reference to the aromatic roots, which were used to perfume clothes, to keep away moths and to flavor spirits. It was said if there was a root of this in the garden, the devil could do nothing. Blooms from May to October.

HEIGHT: To 2 feet.

COLOR: Orange, yellow, red. One fine variety, 'Mrs. Bradshaw,' has large, double scarlet flowers for many weeks.

LOCATION: Sun, half sun.

SOIL: Rich, light soil, well drained.

PROPAGATION: By plant division and seed.

USES: A hardy plant for the border. A good cut flower.

CULTURAL HINTS: Keep moist during the growing season, but in winter plants must not become too wet and soggy. Feed manure in the spring.

FLOWERS THAT START IN SUMMER

CATMINT (*Nepeta mussinii*).
Mint Family
The name *Nepeta* comes from the Etrurian city Nepete, where this plant grew in abundance. It bears a profusion of lavender-blue flowers in loose clusters in June and intermittently through the summer. The silver-gray foliage is attractive, too. Especially appealing when grown with Iceland poppies and madonna lilies. This plant, when chewed, was said to make meek and timid persons fierce and courageous!

HEIGHT: 1 to 1½ feet.

COLOR: Lavender-blue.

LOCATION: Full sun. Dry.

SOIL: Well-drained garden soil on the light side.

PROPAGATION: Cuttings root rapidly any time in June and July. Division of roots. Also sow seed.

USES: In front of the perennial border, on top of a dry wall, as an edging plant. A good ground cover.

CULTURAL HINTS: Feed regularly with a balanced plant food. For best growth and bloom divide the old clumps every other spring.

▲

LILY-OF-THE-VALLEY (*Convallaria majalis*). Lily Family
A flower cherished by young and old that flourishes wild all over Europe, from Italy to Lapland. It was considered the special flower of Ostara, the Norse Goddess of the Dawn. Once used as an ingredient of love potions, the leaves and flowers produce a drug used medicinally today; the white underground stems contain a dangerous poison.

HEIGHT: To 10 inches.
COLOR: White.
LOCATION: Cool, shaded spot.
SOIL: Moderately rich.
PROPAGATION: Readily started from division of the clumps.
USES: Shady parts of the border or rock garden. Excellent as cut flowers for corsages and small bouquets.
FRAGRANT. Delicately scented.
CULTURAL HINTS: Every few years it is necessary to dig the clumps and divide the roots. Be sure the plants are kept moist at all times. Enrich with manure annually in the spring.

MAIDEN PINK (*Dianthus deltoides*). Pink Family
Deliciously fragrant flowers with slightly fringed petals emerge from mats of slender blue-green leaves. Used by the Spaniards in ancient times to give a spicy flavor to beverages. Gerard says, "The conserve made of the floures doth comfort the heart." A plant for everyone and for every peren-

nial garden. The Greek name means "Jove's flower."

◄

HEIGHT: 6 to 10 inches.
COLOR: Pink, white, also a bright, red and a deep purplish variety.
LOCATION: Full sun.
SOIL: Light and sandy, rich and well-drained. Not acid.
PROPAGATION: Flowers the second season from seed.
USES: Delightful in bouquets, for the border, for the rock garden, and as a ground cover in full sun.
FRAGRANT. Sweet, spicy scent.
CULTURAL HINTS: Feed in the spring with lime. Grow in alkaline soil.

CORNFLOWER; MOUNTAIN BLUET (*Centaurea montana*). Composite Family
Windblown, shaggy flowers unfold in spring, and off and on all summer. Flowers are suggestive of a loosely put together thistle blossom. Foliage is gray-green. The plant attracts countless butterflies. Native of North America, North Africa, Europe and Chile. In olden times painters used to prepare a blue color from the petals.

HEIGHT: 2 feet.
COLOR: Blue.
LOCATION: Full sun.
SOIL: Ordinary well-cultivated garden soil. Must have good drainage.
PROPAGATION: Roots spread rapidly and plant may be divided in the spring. Also does well grown from seed.

▼

USES: Excellent border plants. For edging. Beautiful as cut flowers.

CULTURAL HINTS: In the spring feed with manure and bone meal. Water in dry spells in summer.

SIBERIAN IRIS (*I. sibirica*). ▶
Iris Family

Flourishes in acid soil with plenty of moisture. Grasslike foliage with pointed tips. Excellent at the edge of a pond, but not in the water. One of the hardiest of the species and easiest to grow. Many early medicines were made with the Iris. It was said to be a fine sedative and that "it provoketh slepe." Iris roots, hung in a barrel of wine, kept it from going stale. The name *Iris*, according to Plutarch, means Eye of Heaven, and was given to the pupil of the eye and to the rainbow.

HEIGHT: To 2 feet.

COLOR: Blue, white, purple, red.

LOCATION: Full sun.

SOIL: Heavy, acid soil.

PROPAGATION: Divide the rhizomes and plant them rather deep. Also grows well from seed. Needs to be separated every three years.

USES: At the border of a slow-moving stream. A moist place in the perennial border. Good as cut flowers.

FRAGRANT. Delicate scent.

CULTURAL HINTS: Don't cultivate too closely around this Iris, as the rhizomes become compacted. Water regularly during the summer. Survives neglect and is long-lived.

CARNATION (*Dianthus caryophyllus*). Pink Family

Raise your own corsages for important occasions. One of the loveliest scents of all for the perennial border. The fragrance drifts over the garden, seeking you out wherever you are. Especially strong after a summer rain or on a sunny day at noon. The white ones are particularly fragrant at dusk.

HEIGHT: 1 to 2½ feet.

COLOR: Pink, red, white.

LOCATION: Full sun and airy location.

SOIL: Warm, well-drained sandy soil, rich in nutrients. Not acid.

PROPAGATION: Grows well from seed, flowering the second season.

USES: Beautiful cut flowers. Adds color and fragrance to the border. Delightful spilling over a stone wall or in the larger chinks.

FRAGRANT. Spicy scent suggestive of cloves.

CULTURAL HINTS: Give a dressing of lime in the spring. If your soil is acid, give lime three times during the summer. Cover with leaves and branches in winter.

PEONY (*Paeonia albiflora*).
Buttercup Family
Peonies have been a favorite for
generations. Not only are the flowers
showy and fragrant, but both these
virtues are further enhanced by the
beauty of the foliage. The earliest
spring shoots are red-hued, and the first
leaves are reddish. These change to
green as the buds develop. A fascinating
plant to watch in the garden. Some
varieties were introduced from Siberia
and China in the early nineteenth
century and developed into superb hybrids by European, particularly French,
growers. Among the best known and
still unexcelled are 'Festiva Maxima'
(1851), 'Walter Faxon' (1904) and
'Philippe Rivoire' (1911).

> HEIGHT: 2 to 3 feet.
> COLOR: Pink, red, white.
> LOCATION: Full sun.
> SOIL: Heavy, rich soil.
> PROPAGATION: Root divisions. Be
sure each division has an "eye," or bud.
> USES: Make a particular show
when planted in a special peony bed.
Fine cut flowers.
> FRAGRANT. Deeply scented.
> CULTURAL HINTS: For huge
blooms leave only the central bud on
each stalk. The more you feed the
plants, the better the blooms. Give
well-rotted manure in the spring. Keep
thoroughly cultivated and weed-free.
Give ample space. Water during the
growing season. Mulch in winter with
leaves and branches.

▼

LUPINE (*Lupinus polyphyllus*). ▶
Pea Family
Tall, majestic spires of this flower lend a
note of drama to the garden. An established plant may have as many as thirty
spikes during a period of a few weeks.
The unusual palmate leaves retain large
drops of dew or rain. Very difficult to
transplant. Once you have a plant
flourishing in your perennial border,
never move it. An ointment made from
the seeds was used by eighteenth-century
ladies "to smooth the face, soften the
features, and make their charms a little
powerful"!

> HEIGHT: 3 to 5 feet.
> COLOR: Blue, purple, white, rose.
> LOCATION: Partial shade or
full sun.
> SOIL: Deep, well-drained acid
soil. Sandy earth is best.
> PROPAGATION: Grows well from
seed sown in the spring.
> USES: Wonderful plants for a
mixed border of perennials. Excellent
for cut flowers.
> CULTURAL HINTS: Feed with very
well-rotted manure or a commercial
fertilizer in the spring. Give winter
protection with a mulch of leaves
and branches. Avoid lime.

DAYLILY (*Hemerocallis*). Lily Family
Plant breeders have extended the
season and varieties of these superb
lily cousins. These old-time popular
favorites are natives of Japan and Central Europe. The Greek name,
"beautiful for a day," refers to the fact
that each flower lasts but a single day.
However, more keep coming. The
blooming period of each variety lasts
several weeks, and some bloom twice
in a season. Moreover, there are some
night-blooming ones, such as *H. citrina*
and its descendant *H.* 'Hyperion,'
which are lovely, fragrant flowers for
city gardens and balconies.

> HEIGHT: 1 to 4 feet.
> COLOR: Yellow, red, apricot,
salmon, pink, mahogany.
> LOCATION: Sun, partial sun.
> SOIL: Rich, well-drained soil.
> PROPAGATION: Slice the roots
apart in March. Also may be started
from seed.

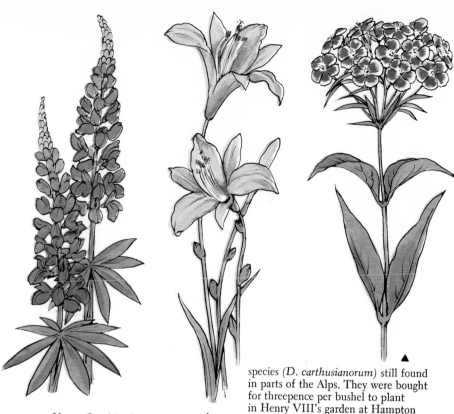

USES: Good in the perennial ▲ border. Excellent in front of shrubs. A stand of these plants by themselves is also very effective. They naturalize well.

FRAGRANT. Subtle scent.

CULTURAL HINTS: Give well-rotted manure each spring, and feed during the summer at intervals. In hot dry weather, if red spider attacks, spray with Malathion or Aramite.

SWEET WILLIAM (*Dianthus barbatus*). Pink Family
An old-fashioned favorite whose dense heads of varicolored flowers spring from brilliant green foliage. One of the oldest of our garden flowers, thought to have been introduced to England by the Carthusian monks about the twelfth century, but now greatly changed and enriched from the wild species (*D. carthusianorum*) still found in parts of the Alps. They were bought for threepence per bushel to plant in Henry VIII's garden at Hampton Court. Thought to be named after St. William of Aquitaine. This is a biennial.

HEIGHT: 8 to 15 inches.

COLOR: Red, pink, purple, white, often bicolored or two-toned.

LOCATION: Full sun.

SOIL: Light, sandy soil, well drained.

PROPAGATION: Flowers the second season when started from seed sown at the beginning of summer. Thin to six inches apart and transplant to permanent places in late September. Established plants will self-sow to some extent.

USES: The brilliant colors add a note of special appeal to the perennial border. Their old-fashioned charm enhances the area where they grow.

FRAGRANT. Sunny-meadow scent.

CULTURAL HINTS: Add lime to the soil in the spring. Cover with a mulch if winters are severe.

and spreads in a tangle. Terminal clusters of flowers, like gold dust, in late spring and summer. The name of the genus comes from the Latin meaning "to sit." This refers to the way the plant "sits" and attaches itself to rocks and walls.

HEIGHT: 1 to 3 inches.
COLOR: Bright yellow.
LOCATION: Sun.
SOIL: Light, sandy soil, well-drained. Ample humus.
PROPAGATION: The tufts divide readily; in fact this plant is apt to spread too readily in small gardens. Has become naturalized in many parts of our Eastern states. Originally from Central Europe and the Alps.
USES: Excellent in rock gardens and on rock walls. A good ground cover for an open location, if kept under control.
CULTURAL HINTS: Feed several times during the summer with a balanced fertilizer.

CARPATHIAN HAREBELL; CARPATHIAN BELLFLOWER
(*Campanula carpatica*). Bellflower Family

Starry flowers rise from solid mats of foliage from June to October. A tough and hardy plant with a long season of bloom. Native to the Mediterranean region. Grows rampantly over the hill-sides of the Greek islands and the Italian Riviera.

HEIGHT: 6 to 15 inches.
COLOR: Blue, white.
LOCATION: Full sun.
SOIL: Rich soil.
PROPAGATION: From seed, division of plants.
USES: Ideal for the border and the rockery. Makes attractive bouquets.
CULTURAL HINTS: Feed in the spring with well-rotted manure and bone meal, working both into the soil around the plants. Give ample room in the bed. Water during summer dry spells.

SEDUM; STONECROP; WALL-PEPPER (*S. acre*).
Orpine Family

Creeps and clings over rocks and walls, where the succulent foliage grows

PYRETHRUM; PAINTED DAISY
(*Chrysanthemum coccineum*). Composite family

From the mist of fernlike foliage emerge single or somewhat double daisylike flowers. Originally introduced from the Caucasus in the nineteenth century. The principal ingredient in the manufacture of Persian insect powder, pyrethrum, is extracted from this plant. As an insecticide, Pyrethrum is increasingly important today, be-cause it is not harmful to the ecology. The powder is made from the flower heads, which are cut as they are about to open, then dried and pulverized.

HEIGHT: 1 to 3 feet.
COLOR: Pink, red shades, white.
LOCATION: Full sun.
SOIL: Rich soil, but not heavy. Perfect drainage important.
PROPAGATION: Division of clumps. Also grows well from seed.
USES: Enhances any bouquet. Fine in the flower border.
FRAGRANT. Subtle scent.
CULTURAL HINTS: Heavy feeders. Give a balanced plant food several times during the summer.

THERMOPSIS (*T. caroliniana*).
Pea Family
Flowers resembling golden lupine
form long racemes in June and July.
Combines artistically with light blue
delphinium for a superb bouquet.
Like the lupine, Thermopsis resists
transplanting, so once it settles and becomes established, don't move it.
Native from North Carolina to
Georgia.
>   HEIGHT: 3 feet or more.
>   COLOR: Canary yellow.
>   LOCATION: Sun.
>   SOIL: Average.
>   PROPAGATION: By seed, which
ripens early and can be planted in
early September.
>   USES: A stately, dignified plant
for the perennial border.
>   CULTURAL HINTS: Stake the
blossoms to prevent wind damage.

▼

SIBERIAN WALLFLOWER
(*Erysimum asperum*). Mustard Family
Brought to England by the Norman
conquerors. Symbol of faithfulness in
adversity. Thrives in a limestone area
and in relative dryness. A most attractive plant for bouquets; a cheery
flower. It comes early in the spring, but
it will not survive, as a rule, much
north of Washington, D.C.
>   HEIGHT: 1 to 3 feet.
>   COLOR: Orange to yellow.
>   LOCATION: Sun.
>   SOIL: Average garden loam.
>   PROPAGATION: Does well when
grown from seed. Also may be propa-
gated by root division.
>   USES: Good in a rock garden or
perennial border. Thrives along banks
in dry areas.
>   FRAGRANT. Sweet scent.
>   CULTURAL HINTS: Be sure to
have good drainage. Cultivate frequently. To increase flowering, feed
during the summer. Divide every
three years.

▼

▲

PINCUSHION FLOWER (*Scabiosa caucasica*). Teasel Family
Shaggy petals surround a fat center resembling a cushion that is stuck full of pins, hence the name. A flower lovely in bouquets, and enriching in the garden, where it blooms over a period of several months.

HEIGHT: 18 to 30 inches.
COLOR: Lavender, blue, white.
LOCATION: Sun, light shade.
SOIL: Light, sandy soil, well drained.
PROPAGATION: Plants divide readily. And although technically a perennial, it is not very long-lived, so seed should be sown afresh every second year.
USES: Ideal flowers for cutting. Popular border plants.
FRAGRANT. Subtle scent.
CULTURAL HINTS: Scatter lime on the soil in the spring. Apply well-rotted manure also in the spring. Feed during the summer.

EVENING-PRIMROSE (*Oenothera biennis*). Evening-primrose Family
At dusk, stand quietly and watch the sepals separate, the petals stir, and the golden blossoms unfold. The poet Keats was "startled by the leap of buds into ripe flowers." (The plant had been introduced from America into England about 1700.) Both roots and leaves are edible. The roots need to be cooked; the leaves may be cooked or

eaten raw. These flowers are host to countless bees and butterflies. They bloom during a period of several weeks.

HEIGHT: 3 to 4 feet.
COLOR: Deep yellow.
LOCATION: Full sun.
SOIL: Rich soil, well-drained.
PROPAGATION: Divide the roots in the spring.
USES: Shows off well when used in groups in front of shrubs. Excellent in the perennial border. A dramatic and effective plant to enhance the garden at dusk.
FRAGRANT. Subtle scent.
CULTURAL HINTS: Feed during the summer with a balanced plant food. Cultivate regularly. Protect the plants during the winter.

CORAL-BELLS (*Heuchera sanguinea*). Saxifrage Family
Airy sprays of tiny bell-shaped flowers rise from a rosette of attractive dark green leaves. Flowers over a long period. An old-time favorite that grows beautifully in front of delphinium, placed here and there in a rose garden, or with white phlox.

HEIGHT: 12 to 15 inches.
COLOR: Coral. Also pink, red and white varieties.
LOCATION: Full sun.
SOIL: Rich soil, well-drained.
PROPAGATION: Divide the plants in the spring.
USES: Makes a charming addition to bouquets. Good in the border.

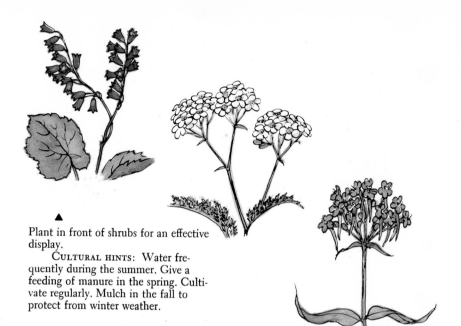

Plant in front of shrubs for an effective display.

CULTURAL HINTS: Water frequently during the summer. Give a feeding of manure in the spring. Cultivate regularly. Mulch in the fall to protect from winter weather.

ACHILLEA; YARROW; ROSY MILFOIL (*A. Millefolium*).
Composite Family
This plant was named after Achilles, who is said to have learned from Chiron, the centaur, how to use it to heal the wounds of his soldiers. A beautiful plant in the garden, delightful in bouquets and in the perennial border, where it enhances the whole area. Grows the world over, from America to New Zealand and the Orient.

HEIGHT: 18 to 24 inches.

COLOR: White, pink, red. Long-flowering variety 'Cerise Queen' is rich cherry red with white center.

LOCATION: Full sun.

SOIL: Average garden loam, well drained.

PROPAGATION: Division of plants. Seeds planted in the spring will flower the following year.

USES: Good for cut flowers. Fine in the perennial border.

FRAGRANT. Foliage is aromatic.

CULTURAL HINTS: Feed bone meal in the spring. Cultivate regularly.

RED VALERIAN; JUPITER'S BEARD (*Centranthus ruber*, formerly *Valeriana coccinea*). Valerian Family
Bright panicles of flowers blossom all season. Ovate leaves to four inches long. Thrives in lime soil, in chinks in old walls, and anywhere hot and dry. The name comes from the Latin word *valere*, meaning "to be strong," and referring to the health-giving properties of the plant. Native to Europe and Southwest Asia.

HEIGHT: To 3 feet.

COLOR: Rose or crimson.

LOCATION: Sun.

SOIL: Light, sandy soil, well-drained.

PROPAGATION: Division of roots, seed; will self-sow in undisturbed soil.

USES: Attractive in the perennial border. A good cut flower.

FRAGRANT. Sweet scent.

CULTURAL HINTS: Keep on the damp side and feed occasionally with a balanced plant food. Cultivate regularly, but watch out for seedlings in late summer.

GARLAND LARKSPUR (*Delphinium cheilanthum*). Buttercup Family
A dramatic and appealing perennial. Individual florets are shaped like horns of plenty. Easy to grow are 'Belladonna' (light blue), 'Bellamosum' (deep blue) and 'Casa Blanca' (white). Blooms almost continually during the summer. *Delphinium* means "dolphin" and refers to the shape of the flowers in bud. The foliage is handsome, the habit more branching than that of the larger and taller Candle or Bee delphiniums; but these Garland hybrids are easier to grow and very colorful.

HEIGHT: 3 to 4 feet.
COLOR: Blue, lavender, white.
LOCATION: Full sun, and where there is good air circulation.
SOIL: Rich, well-drained soil that is light and friable and somewhat sandy. Prefers it slightly alkaline.
PROPAGATION: Clumps may be divided every three years or so. Also grows well from seed, flowering the following year.
USES: A must for the perennial border. Accent plants against a fence or shrub background. Good for cut flowers.

CULTURAL HINTS: Keep the plants well watered. A summertime mulch helps maintain damp soil. Stake the blossoms. For continuous bloom cut the plants back after the first flowering.

COREOPSIS; TICKSEED (*C. grandiflora*). Composite Family
A foolproof plant, fine for beginners. Golden flowers vibrant in the sun invite picking. Will flower almost all summer. Effective when planted with Shasta daisies and delphiniums. Foliage is rather thin, so plant it among well-foliaged plants.

HEIGHT: 18 to 24 inches.
COLOR: Yellow.
LOCATION: Full sun.
SOIL: Adapts to every kind of soil, but does best in rich, well-drained earth.
PROPAGATION: Careful division of plants in spring. Flowers the following year from spring-sown seed.
USES: A showy plant for the border. Appealing cut flowers.
CULTURAL HINTS: Keep the soil moist in summer. Keep well cultivated and feed a balanced fertilizer. Pick off faded flowers for all-summer bloom.

ASTER (*A. frikartii* 'Wonder of Staffa'). Composite Family
Unusual in that the plant sends up an abundance of flowers from June to November, even after a frost or two. Not too often seen in gardens, and deserves more attention, since it blooms through the heat of the summer well before other asters are out. Aster means star, and refers to the starry effect of the many petals. This variety has violet-blue petals and a gold center, and often measures two inches across—not infrequently three inches.

HEIGHT: 1½ to 2 feet.
COLOR: Violet-blue.
LOCATION: Sun, partial sun.
SOIL: Adapts to every kind of soil, but does best with rich earth. Must have fine drainage.

PROPAGATION: Seeds planted in the spring will bring bloom the following year. Divide clumps in the spring, at least every third year.

USES: Fine border plant. Effective in front of shrubs in drifts. Can complement early-flowering low-growing chrysanthemums.

FRAGRANT. Slightly scented.

CULTURAL HINTS: Water frequently during the summer, especially during dry spells. Feed well-rotted manure in the spring. It is sometimes bothered by root aphids, which can be eradicated by nicotine insecticides poured deeply over the soil. Mulch during the winter.

GLOBEFLOWER (*Trollius europaeus*). Buttercup Family
A glorified Buttercup, round and fat. Thrives in dampness at the edge of sunny bogs and ponds. A native of Scotland, the north of England and Scandinavia, where the damp, rainy weather is greatly to its liking. Made into wreaths and garlands, it adorned the doorways of cottages. Fragrant when drying, and used in Sweden to strew floors on holidays. The name originated from the old German word ▶ *trol*, meaning spherical.

HEIGHT: 1 to 2 feet.

COLOR: Yellow.

LOCATION: Full or partial sun; does best in damp areas.

SOIL: Rich, moist soil.

PROPAGATION: Divide the plants right after flowering.

USES: Adapts to the perennial border. Does well in a wildflower garden, along a stream or brook.

CULTURAL HINTS: Water frequently during the summer. Feed regularly.

AGAPANTHUS; AFRICAN LILY; ▶
LILY OF THE NILE (*A. africanus*).
Lily Family*
This tall and stately flower is a spectacular addition to the perennial border. *Agapanthus*, from the Greek,

means "love flower." Often called Blue Lily of the Nile. Best in Southern gardens. In the North, grow in tubs, where it will produce many flowers in July and August. Winter in the basement, in any frost-free place that is not too dark. Blooms from late spring to fall. Native of South Africa.

HEIGHT: To 30 inches, taller in the South.

COLOR: Blue.

LOCATION: Full sun, well-protected area.

SOIL: Rich soil and good drainage.

PROPAGATION: Divide the rhizomes; soak in water to help you separate them.

USES: Excellent border plant where winters are mild. Makes a fine show when planted in front of shrubs. Also good for cut flowers.

CULTURAL HINTS: Give plenty of water during the growing season. Feed regularly with liquid manure. In the South, mulch in winter to protect from cold.

*Now transferred by some botanists to the new family *Alliaceae* (Allium Family).

CANTERBURY BELLS (*Campanula medium, C. calycanthema*). Bellflower Family

These charming bell-shaped flowers were Grandmother's favorite. The plant, native to the Mediterranean area, bears a pyramid of blooms. Actually a biennial, it is a delicate and effective addition to the flower border. In our Northeastern states it is lovely for June weddings. The flowers resemble in shape the small bells with which the Canterbury pilgrims adorned their horses. The form *calycanthema* is double; the blossom looks like a cup and saucer.

HEIGHT: 2 to 4 feet.

COLOR: Pink, blue, lavender, white.

LOCATION: Sun.

SOIL: Rich soil.

PROPAGATION: From divisions or from seed.

USES: Ideal for the border. Make fine cut flowers.

CULTURAL HINTS: Give ample room. In the spring, feed well-rotted manure and bone meal. Keep moist. Stake to prevent wind and rain damage.

MALTESE CROSS; JERUSALEM CROSS (*Lychnis chalcedonica*). Pink Family

Tall flower native to Russia, as far north as Siberia. Sometimes called Scarlet Lightning. Withstands drought. Introduced to Europe at the time of the Crusades. It is believed to have been brought back toFrance by Louis IX on his return from the Holy Land. The genus name is from a Greek word meaning "lamp."

HEIGHT: 2½ to 3½ feet.

COLOR: Vermilion, scarlet, flesh-colored, white.

LOCATION: Full sun.

SOIL: Light, sandy soil, well fertilized.

PROPAGATION: Seed or plant divisions in the spring. Seedlings take one or two years to flower.

USES: A fine border plant. Excellent for cut flowers.

CULTURAL HINTS: Keep on the dry side. Stake the flower stalks.

PENSTEMON; BEARDTONGUE (*P. hartwegii*). Snapdragon Family

Like many-colored cathedral spires in your garden. Especially fine in the South. Introduced into Britain during the eighteenth century, it was originally found in the mountains of Mexico by early explorers. *Penstemon*, from the

◀ Greek, means "with five stamens," and refers to the structure of the blossom.

HEIGHT: To 2 feet; higher in the South.

COLOR: Lilac, purple, white, pink, cherry.

LOCATION: Sun, half sun.

SOIL: Light, sandy soil, well drained; add a little fertilizer.

PROPAGATION: Divide the plants in early fall. Sow seeds in the spring.

USES: A fine border plant. Good cut flowers.

CULTURAL HINTS: Give a winter covering in the North. Keep well watered during the summer. Feed regularly.

FOXGLOVE; WITCH'S THIMBLES
(*Digitalis purpurea*). Snapdragon Family

The ancient Druids liked this plant because the flower resembled a priest's miter. The common name "Witch's Thimbles" refers to the flower's re-

semblance also to a long, narrow thimble. It would fit a witch's slim finger well! The name *Digitalis*, from the Latin, means "finger of a glove." This is a biennial. Foxglove is the source of the valuable drug digitalis, which is an important heart medicine. In olden times it had many other medicinal uses.

HEIGHT: 2 to 4 feet.

COLOR: White, purple, pink.

LOCATION: Full sun, half sun.

SOIL: Rich, moist soil with plenty of humus. The soil should be acid and well drained.

PROPAGATION: Start from seed sown early in the summer. Will flower the following season.

CULTURAL HINTS: Add peat moss from time to time. Keep the soil acid. A light summer mulch will maintain moist earth. Water frequently. Give a winter mulch of leaves and branches.

GARDEN-HELIOTROPE; ALLHEAL; ST. GEORGE'S-HERB; COMMON VALERIAN (*Valeriana officinalis*). Valerian Family

◀ If you wish to stir up a lion or the family cat, toss a sprig of Garden-Heliotrope his way. Cats are greatly attracted by the roots and lower stems of this charming old-fashioned plant; and some protection for it such as strong wire netting, may be desirable. Used medicinally years ago and today as well. Small, fragrant flowers, borne in flat terminal clusters, are soft and furry to touch.

HEIGHT: 2 to 5 feet.

COLOR: Rose-tinted white flowers in June–July.

LOCATION: Half sun, full sun.

SOIL: Average garden loam, well drained.

PROPAGATION: By division or from seed; spreads rapidly.

USES: A good border plant. Fine for cut flowers.

FRAGRANT. A clean, lovely scent.

CULTURAL HINTS: Water frequently. Stake the flowers to prevent wind damage. Till the surface of the soil.

GAS PLANT; BURNING BUSH; DITTANY; FRAXINELLA (*Dictamnus fraxinella, D. albus*). Rue Family Blossoms and seedpods exude a gas that, when lit, burns in a bright flash that is harmless to the plant. This unusual flower was described in medieval days as being a "verie rare galant plant." It is, indeed, exotic and well worth growing. Native of Central and Southern Europe and China.

HEIGHT: 2 to 3 feet.

COLOR: White, pink, red-brown, rose-purple.

LOCATION: Full sun and open area.

SOIL: Rich, heavy soil.

PROPAGATION: Start from seed; cover with about an inch of soil. Generally a long-lived plant where properly situated.

USES: Does well in a permanent location in the perennial bed. Good for cut flowers.

FRAGRANT. Foliage and flowers exude a strong lemon scent.

CULTURAL HINTS: Does not transplant well. Keep soil loose and weeds down. Feed well-rotted manure in the spring.

THALICTRUM; MEADOW-RUE (*T. aquilegifolium*). Buttercup Family Tall, graceful plants with columbine-like foliage and myriads of feathery flowers in early summer. In olden days it was believed that to lay a newborn child on a pillow stuffed with Meadow-Rue flowers was to ensure for the child wealth, health and happiness for life.

HEIGHT: To 3 feet.

COLOR: There are white, pink, pale yellow, and lavender varieties; the color is in the crowded stamens and sepals.

LOCATION: Partial shade or full sun.

SOIL: Well-drained garden loam with leafmold and peat moss.

PROPAGATION: Start from seed or by division in the spring.

USES: Lovely in bouquets. Attractive addition to the border; perhaps best growing freely, as if naturalized, in low, woodsy places or beside paths on the margins of open woods.

FRAGRANT. Subtle scent.

CULTURAL HINTS: Keep moderately moist and cultivate regularly. Give a winter mulch as a protection against cold weather.

MEADOWSWEET; FLORISTS' SPIREA (*Astilbe japonica*). Saxifrage Family Blossoms are soft and plumy, with the scent of new-mown hay. This fine plant thrives in moist areas near water. The broad spires of snowy bloom appear from June to August. There are a number of hybrid Astilbes now offered by nurseries in shades of pink, rose, coral, carmine and white, and they are among the most satisfactory perennials, especially for damp woodsy places.

HEIGHT: 1½ to 3 feet.

COLOR: White.

LOCATION: Full sun, part shade. Does best near water.

SOIL: Rich soil.

PROPAGATION: Division of roots. Also plant seeds in the spring.

USES: A good plant for the perennial border. Fine in porch boxes and urns. Excellent for bouquets.

FRAGRANT. Lovely haunting scent.

CULTURAL HINTS: Mulch in summer to keep the roots damp. Water frequently and feed regularly.

SOIL: Rich soil, very acid.

PROPAGATION: Start from divisions and also from seed.

USES: A spectacular flower for accents along a stream or a moist border. Good as a cut flower.

FRAGRANT. A delicate scent.

CULTURAL HINTS: Don't cultivate around the roots, as they are very shallow.

VERBENA *(V. rigida)*. Verbena ▶ Family

From southern Brazil, this handsome, appealing perennial, little grown, deserves more attention. The angular-growing plant has rough, sharply saw-edged leaves, and produces fairly showy flowers all summer. Cut blossoms last a week in water.

HEIGHT: 18 to 24 inches.

COLOR: Purple or rose-magenta; also now comes in white.

LOCATION: Full sun, half sun.

SOIL: Average garden loam.

PROPAGATION: By division of plants and grows well from seed; also spreads by creeping stems.

USES: Effective in a drift in the flower border or in front of shrubs.

CULTURAL HINTS: Feed in the spring and cultivate regularly during the summer.

JAPANESE IRIS *(I. kaempferi)*. Iris ▶ Family

In olden days called Ground Rainbow —a promise that beauty on earth would never end. The dramatic flowers are often nearly a foot across. Plant needs replacing every two or three years.

HEIGHT: 2 to 3½ feet.

COLOR: Blue, purple, white, many elaborate cultivars.

LOCATION: Likes full sun and moist soil. Does well at the edge of sunny bogs or quiet streams in swamp conditions.

ROSE CAMPION (*Lychnis coronaria*).
Pink Family
Lychnis comes from the Greek, meaning "lamp," and refers to the glowing
flowers. Velvety silver-gray leaves are
lovely to stroke. The combination of
cerise blossoms and gray foliage is most ▶
attractive. A useful plant for dry seashore locations as it withstands drought
very well.

    HEIGHT: To 2 feet.
    COLOR: Cerise, white.
    LOCATION: Full sun.
    SOIL: Light, sandy soil, well-
drained, well fertilized.
    PROPAGATION: By plant division
or seeds sown in spring. Under good
conditions plants often self-sow.
    USES: A splendid plant for the
border. Excellent as cut flowers.
    CULTURAL HINTS: Keep on the
dry side. Grow where drainage is
perfect.

TRAILING CUP-FLOWER   ▶
(*Nierembergia rivularis, N. repens
rivularis*). Nightshade Family
A plant for a moist area, where it never
stops opening its upward-facing
creamy cups all summer long. The
name Nierembergia commemorates
Juan E. Nieremberg, a Spanish natural
historian. The plant was introduced to
England from Spain in 1786, but it
came originally from Argentina.
    HEIGHT: 2 to 5 inches, creeping
and mat-forming.
    COLOR: Creamy white.
    LOCATION: Full sun.
    SOIL: Light loam, never really
dry, except in winter.
    PROPAGATION: Grows from seed,
also by division, in the spring.
    USES: Excellent plant for the
front of the perennial border. Fine in
the rock garden or trailing down a
bank.
    CULTURAL HINTS: Keep moist
with frequent watering all summer.
Divide the clumps every third or fourth
year.

ICELAND POPPY (*Papaver nudi-
caule*). Poppy Family
An eighteenth-century introduction
from Siberia. Beautiful in indoor
bouquets and lasts well if the stem tips
are burned before being put in water.
These crisp-petaled, two-and-one-half-
inch-wide flowers have a freshly pressed
look which is most appealing. A biennial or short-lived perennial, hence new
plants should be kept coming on. If
naturalized over a wide area it will
reseed itself in a gratifying manner.
    HEIGHT: 1 to 2 feet.
    COLOR: Lemon, orange, white,
red.
    LOCATION: Full sun.
    SOIL: Average garden loam with
plenty of humus.
    PROPAGATION: Start from seed
sown in the spring. Young plants will
winter over and bloom the following
summer.

USES: A fine border plant, useful in the rockery. Excellent naturalizers in open places.

FRAGRANT. Sweetly scented like a jonquil, especially morning and evening.

CULTURAL HINTS: Keep the faded flowers picked for a long period of bloom. Enrich the soil by feeding regularly. Protect in the winter with a mulch.

▼

CORFU LILY; PLANTAIN LILY (*Hosta plantaginea*). Lily Family
From China and Japan. Blooms for weeks in late sumer and early fall, with many trumpet-shaped flowers opening in succession. The ribbed basal leaves are much sought after for arrangements. The name *Hosta* is for N. T. Host, an Austrian botanist. The plants have sturdy roots and live many years in the garden. Very easy for beginners if not allowed to suffer drought.

HEIGHT: 1½ to 2 feet.

COLOR: White, lavender, lavender-blue.

LOCATION: Full sun, part shade.

SOIL: Deep, rich, well-drained soil. If kept damp, will grow in many different kinds of soil.

PROPAGATION: Divide the roots or start from seed.

USES: Popular in borders and old-fashioned gardens.

FRAGRANT. Penetrating scent. ▶

CULTURAL HINTS: Cultivate regularly and feed often with a well-balanced fertilizer. Mulch lightly during the winter.

STOKESIA (*S. Laevis*). Composite Family
Tough and hardy, this plant is fine for those new to gardening. Shaggy cornflowerlike blossoms, fascinating under a magnifying glass, bloom for a long season. Named for Jonathan Stokes, an English botanist. Will stand drought.

HEIGHT: 12 to 18 inches.

COLOR: Lavender, blue, white, rose.

LOCATION: Full sun.

SOIL: Light, sandy soil, well drained.

PROPAGATION: Sow seed in the spring.

USES: A fine border plant. Does well in a greenhouse. Cut flowers are attractive and long-lasting.

FRAGRANT. Lovely scent.

CULTURAL HINTS: Apply well-rotted manure in the spring and feed during the summer.

▼

▲ ▲

LAVENDER *(Lavandula officinalis)*.
Mint Family
Both blossoms and feltlike leaves have
a lasting fragrance. Native from India
to the Canary Islands. Grows on dry,
stony land. Old herbals say it heals
"them that use to swoune much." The
genus name, *Lavandula,* is from the
Latin meaning "to wash," because the
ancients used it to perfume their baths.
Distilling the oil of lavender for perfume is a considerable industry in southern France and Spain today.
     HEIGHT: To 3 feet.
     COLOR: Lavender-blue.
     LOCATION: Full sun.
     SOIL: Light, stony, and limy, but
with some humus.
     PROPAGATION: Start from seed
sown in the spring. Keep young plants
shaded.
     USES: Well liked as a border
plant. Sometimes used as a low hedge.
Good in dry areas such as banks. Excellent as cut flowers. Dry the blossoms
for sachets.
     FRAGRANT. Very fragrant foliage
and flowers.
     CULTURAL HINTS: Mulch during
the winter to protect from cold. Feed
during the summer. Clip back lightly
after flowering.

BALLOONFLOWER *(Platycodon
grandiflorum)*. Bellflower Family
One of the easiest and best. The name
Platycodon is from the Greek meaning

"broad bell," and is suggested by the
shape of the flower. The buds are
like small balloons, hence the popular
name. The roots were once used as
a substitute for ginseng, a famous and
valuable panacea of the Orient.
     HEIGHT: Usually 1 to 2½ feet;
established plants often much higher.
     COLOR: Blue, lavender, purple,
white.
     LOCATION: Sun, semishade.
     SOIL: Medium, sandy soil, loose
but containing some humus. Must
be well drained.
     PROPAGATION: Start from seeds
sown in spring.
     USES: Fine as cut flowers. Lends
a note of pure blue to the summer
garden. The paler-colored varieties are
often markedly veined.
     CULTURAL HINTS: In the spring,
cultivate the area carefully because
the plants appear late. Stake the stems
and clip the spent flowers to stimulate
prolonged blooming.

LIMONIUM; STATICE *(L. lati-
folium)*. Plumbago Family
This plant, also called Sea Lavender,
brings a violet mist to the garden.
Flourishes at the seashore. This was
popular in Tudor times in the old-
fashioned knot gardens, where it was
trimmed to shape.
     HEIGHT: 1 to 2 feet.
     COLOR: Violet; and modern
horticultural forms in white, lavender.

LOCATION: Full sun.

SOIL: Light, sandy soil with good drainage.

PROPAGATION: Start new plants by division or from seed.

USES: A fine edging plant for walks and drives. Useful in the rock garden. Dry it for winter bouquets.

CULTURAL HINTS: Keep on the dry side. Feed occasionally with a balanced plant food. ◀

BABY'S-BREATH; CHALK PLANT
(*Gypsophila paniculata*). Pink Family
This many-branched plant forms a soft, misty cloud in your garden because of the clusters of myriad tiny florets that cover it. Called in Italy *velo disposa*, bridal veil. Prefers a lime soil. Native to Asia and Europe.

HEIGHT: 2 to 3 feet.

COLOR: White. Also pale pink and rosy pink forms.

LOCATION: Full sun and part shade.

SOIL: Well-drained average garden loam.

PROPAGATION: Start new plants from seed or from July cuttings inserted in sandy soil in a coldframe.

USES: Adds a light and airy feeling to the perennial border. Popular as a cut flower. Dries well for winter bouquets.

▼

CULTURAL HINTS: Spread lime about the roots from time to time during the summer. Large clumps can be supported by a ring of thin bamboo stakes interlaced with Twistems or twine.

BLANKETFLOWER (*Gaillardia aristata*) Composite Family
Gay Mexican-blanket colors. Likes plenty of space, but has rather skimpy foliage, so for garden effect it is often well to plant near more abundantly leaved plants. Genus name is for M. Gaillard de Marentonneau, a French patron of botany. This native of North America grows wild by the mile in the pastures of Nebraska, creating the effect of a vast Persian carpet.

HEIGHT: 1½ to 3 feet.

COLOR: Red, orange, yellow.

LOCATION: Full sun.

SOIL: Light and well-drained soil, reasonably rich.

PROPAGATION: Plant divisions in the spring. Seeds may be sown as soon as the frost is out of the ground, but will not always produce flowers exactly resembling the parent.

USES: Popular in the border. Does well in wild or naturalized areas.

CULTURAL HINTS: Fertilize regularly during the summer. Cultivate frequently.

▼

▲

SHOWY SEDUM *(S. spectabile)*.
Orpine Family
Gray-green leaves, thick and succulent,
are of unusual form and beauty. Flat
clusters of pink or white or deep
rose flower heads remain in bloom for
weeks, from August on, where it is hot
and dry. This is a plant of Japanese
origin. Attracts butterflies.

HEIGHT: 12 to 18 inches.
COLOR: Various shades of pink.
LOCATION: Full sun.
SOIL: Light, sandy soil, well
drained.
PROPAGATION: Start new plants
from division of tufts in the early
spring.
USES: An excellent ground cover
for an open location. An interesting
plant to try to naturalize; does well
in cities.
FRAGRANT. Subtle scent.
CULTURAL HINTS: Keep weeds
removed. Cultivate regularly and feed
occasionally with a balanced plant food.
Likes shallow soil.

CAMOMILE *(Anthemis nobilis)*.
Composite Family
Daisylike flowers rise up from heavily
scented low, feathery foliage. Grow
hot and dry and treat roughly. The
source of the tea of Peter Rabbit fame!
Some years ago dried flower heads
were used medicinally as a tonic and
in treating fevers.

HEIGHT: 1 foot when in bloom;
the foliage is like a ground cover.

COLOR: Yellow.
LOCATION: Full sun, partial
shade.
SOIL: Light, well-drained, sandy
soil.
PROPAGATION: Easily raised from
seed sown outdoors in the spring. Also
by division of old plants.
USES: An aromatic ground cover.
Very fragrant when crushed. Makes a
delicious tea.
FRAGRANT. The foliage and
flowers are aromatic.
CULTURAL HINTS: This plant
needs no special care or food.

▼

VERONICA *(V. longifolia subsessilus)*.
Snapdragon Family
Tall spikes are studded with feathery
blossoms that last a long time in the
garden. Markings resemble those on
the sacred handkerchief of St. Veronica,
hence the name. A very popular, easy-
to-grow plant, welcomed by beginning
gardeners.

HEIGHT: 1½ to 3 feet.
COLOR: Blue—a true blue.
LOCATION: Full sun, part shade.
SOIL: Adapts to many kinds
of soil.
PROPAGATION: Start from
divisions in the spring; also from seed.
USES: Appealing in an all-blue
garden. Adds a fine note here and there
in the perennial border.
CULTURAL HINTS: Water occa-

▲

sionally during the summer. Feed regularly. Stake the flower heads to protect from wind and rain damage.

SUMMER PHLOX (*P. paniculata*). Phlox Family
Native of North America. Give plenty of elbow room in the bed. The massive flower panicles on their tall stalks lend a note of great dignity to the midsummer garden. Every perennial border should have some Phlox. The mauve variety was introduced into cultivation by an English garden authority, Dr. James Sherrard, who grew it in his garden at Eltham in the eighteenth century. There are now over a hundred varieties.
HEIGHT: 2 to 4 feet.

▲

COLOR: Pinks, reds, lavenders, in many tones; also white.
LOCATION: Full sun, partial sun.
SOIL: Rich soil, but not over-damp. Too much dampness tends to cause mildew and fungous rust of stems and leaves; these conditions, however, can be controlled by dusting with sulphur.
PROPAGATION: By divisions made in the spring or autumn; also by seed sown in spring.
USES: Fine in the perennial border. Also makes attractive cut flowers for large bouquets.
FRAGRANT. Haunting sweet scent, especially at dusk.
CULTURAL HINTS: A mulch of manure during the summer is beneficial. Give ample plant food. Water frequently.

HOLLYHOCK *(Althaea rosea)*.
Mallow Family
An old-fashioned favorite, especially in Colonial gardens, and a modern delight. Beloved by bees. Has been grown extensively in England since the fifteenth century. Originally cultivated in China during the fifth or sixth century; the Chinese still eat the flowers today as a special culinary delicacy. In the early nineteenth century the plant was grown on a large scale to use the stem fibers as hemp. Also the plant provided a blue die. A biennial that self-sows so freely that it is, in effect, a perennial.

HEIGHT: 5 to 8 feet.
COLOR: Pink, maroon, yellow, red, white.
LOCATION: Sun and good air circulation.
SOIL: Average.
PROPAGATION: Sow seeds in July and August for blooms the following year.
USES: As a background plant in the perennial border. Lovely along a fence. Grow singly in a row for a spectacular effect. The blossoms are attractive floating in a shallow bowl on the dining table.

▼

CULTURAL HINTS: In setting out, place the crowns of the plants a little below the soil surface. These plants need no regular feeding. The fungous disease puccinia malvacearum can be ruinous, covering the plants with rust-colored spores. Spray, using a fine nozzle, with sulphide of potassium or the commercial preparations Fermate or Zineb, at frequent intervals.

BELLFLOWER *(Campanula persicifolia)*. Bellflower Family
The star-shaped flowers clustering up and down the stalks open to reveal three-pronged white stigmas. Native to the Mediterranean area. These garden bells were used in gargles and lotions in olden days and the roots were often eaten in salads. Distilled water extracted from the whole plant was said to make the complexion clear. There are white forms and double forms; also a clear light blue variety called 'Telham Beauty.' The variety 'Grandiflora' has the largest blossoms of all.

HEIGHT: 1 to 3 feet.
COLOR: Purple, blue, white.
LOCATION: Full sun.
SOIL: Very rich soil.
PROPAGATION: Division or seed.
USES: Ideal in the border.
CULTURAL HINTS: Feed in the spring with well-rotted manure and bone meal, and three or four times during the summer at regular intervals with a balanced plant food. Keep
◄ moist. Mulch in winter to protect from cold.

GLOBE THISTLE *(Echinops ritro)*.
Composite Family
From fierce, spiny, feltlike foliage emerge quantities of attractive lavender spherical flowers. *Echinops,* from the Greek, meaning "like a hedgehog," refers to the spine-tipped and much divided leaves. Blooms from early July until the end of September. A host to bees and butterflies all summer long. A native plant from Spain to Asia Minor and Siberia.

HEIGHT: 1 to 3 feet.
COLOR: Blue-lavender.
LOCATION: Full sun.
SOIL: Any soil, but must have good drainage.
PROPAGATION: From divisions made in the spring, or from seed.
USES: Background in the perennial border. Dry the blossoms for winter bouquets.
CULTURAL HINTS: Give ample ▶ space for individual plants and keep fairly dry.

SIDALCEA (S. malvaeflora).
Mallow Family
Often called Miniature Hollyhock or Checkerbloom, and native to Colorado and California. The flowers welcome picking and keep coming. The plant is appreciated for its long-blooming period (late June to mid-September), and for the lovely bouquets the blossom stalks create.
HEIGHT: 2 to 3 feet.
COLOR: Deep pink, pale pink.
LOCATION: Full sun.
SOIL: Well-drained, rich, sandy soil.
PROPAGATION: By seeds or division of roots.
USES: Good in the flower border. Also naturalizes readily in wild areas.
CULTURAL HINTS: Keep the plants moist and feed regularly. ▶

VERBASCUM (V. olympicum).
Snapdragon Family
Introduced to the United States from England; a native of Europe. Thrives in drought. The early Romans dipped the stalks in tallow and burned them as torches. These flowers have a long season of bloom. The plant is a biennial. The woolly and downy gray-green foliage is as attractive as the showy and dramatic blossoms. The European peasants used to put the thick leaves into their shoes for winter warmth.
HEIGHT: 5 to 6 feet.
COLOR: Yellow, amber, white. ▶

LOCATION: Full sun.
SOIL: Adapts to all kinds of soil.
PROPAGATION: By plant division and from seed sown in spring.
USES: Appropriate in a semiwild area. Good in the back of the perennial border if space is large and roomy.
CULTURAL HINTS: Set out young plants only when the spring earth has warmed up.

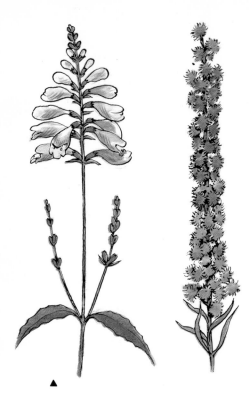

◀ GAY-FEATHER; BLAZING STAR
(Liatris scariosa). Composite Family
The foliage resembles that of the
Easter lily. Clusters of small florets
bloom from the top down. Attracts
bees and butterflies. The tall flower
spikes appear continually in August and
September. Native of Eastern and
Southern North America, also of the
Midwestern prairies.
>HEIGHT: 3 to 5 feet.
>COLOR: Violet-purple, also a
good white form.
>LOCATION: Partial sun.
>SOIL: Adapts to every soil.
>PROPAGATION: Plant divisions or
seed sown in spring.
>USES: Best grown in masses well
at the back of the perennial bed, or
in a naturalized area. Also thrives in
city gardens.
>CULTURAL HINTS: Keep the
plants moist.

CUTLEAF CONEFLOWER;
GOLDEN GLOW *(Rudbeckia
laciniata).* Composite Family
Found in old-fashioned gardens and
on farms, where it is a favorite. The
attractive flower, in full bloom, is like a
small open umbrella with a pompon
on top. Native of North America. The
variety *hortensis* is the popular Golden
Glow, tall and erect, with profuse
double flowers in spherical heads.

▼

▲

FALSE DRAGONHEAD;
OBEDIENT PLANT
(Physostegia virginiana). Mint Family
Often called Obedient Plant because
the individual flowers remain at any
angle to which you turn them. This
plant is excellent in the garden because
of its long season of bloom. The Greek
name means "bladder," and is suggested by the inflated fruiting calyx. A
most reliable, trouble-free plant.
>HEIGHT: 3 to 4 feet.
>COLOR: Lilac, rosy pink, white.
>LOCATION: Partially shaded area.
A moist spot is essential. A stream bank
is to its liking.
>SOIL: Adapts to most soils.
>PROPAGATION: Plant divisions or
seed sown in spring.
>USES: Good as a cut flower Can
be naturalized in moist low woods.
>CULTURAL HINTS: Keep moist at
all times. Divide and transplant every
third year.

HEIGHT: 3 to 6 feet.
COLOR: Gold.
LOCATION: Full sun. Prefers a moist situation, but will also flourish where it is dry.
SOIL: Adapts to just about every soil.
PROPAGATION: By division of roots or seed sown in spring.
USES: Grow in clusters for showy and spectacular effects.
CULTURAL HINTS: Support the plants to protect them from wind and storms. Cultivate regularly. Feed occasionally.

HELEN'S FLOWER (*Helenium autumnale*). Composite Family
Named for Helen of Troy. Looks well at the back of the bed or against shrubs. Comes in all the tawny autumn shades and is compatible with all fall foliage colors. Native to Mexico and adjacent North American areas in swampy places.
HEIGHT: 3 to 6 feet.
COLOR: Gold, red, copper.
LOCATION: Full sun.
SOIL: Average soil, on the damp side.
PROPAGATION: Plant division, seed sown in spring.
USES: Good border plants. Does

▼

well among shrubbery. Fine for cut flowers.
CULTURAL HINTS: Water frequently. Keep well cultivated.

MICHAELMAS DAISY (*Aster novi-belgi*). Composite Family
This flower breathes the essence of fall days, days of lavender mists and flamboyant foliage across the landscape. Each many-petaled blossom with a tufted center brings the drama of the season to your flower bed. Given rich soil and fertilizer, it is spectacular. This was originally a species of Aster native to New York, but it was long ago hybridized with the New England Aster and others to produce numerous forms; so you must rely on your nurseryman's catalogue for special kinds you may want.
HEIGHT: 2½ to 3 feet.
COLOR: Pink, blue, white, lavender, purple.
LOCATION: Full sun, partial shade.
SOIL: Will grow in average soil, but does best in rich earth.
PROPAGATION: By divisions made from old clumps. Seed sown in spring one year produces flowers the next.
USES: A fine background plant for the perennial border. Grow along a fence, or in front of tall evergreens. Attractive as cut flowers.
CULTURAL HINTS: Feed well-rotted manure early in the spring.

▼

▲

SHASTA DAISY (*Chrysanthemum maximum* variety). Composite Family
Variety 'Mount Shasta,' with a crested center, often has blooms four inches across; it is one of Burbank's signal creations. Flowers for many weeks. This stately plant brings a glow of pure white to the garden and a note of dignity. A must for everyone. Has a tendency to die out, so is best treated like a biennial. A native of the Pyrenees. Often called the Moon Daisy.
HEIGHT: 2 to 3 feet.
COLOR: Pure white.
LOCATION: Full sun.
SOIL: Fertile but not heavy.
PROPAGATION: From clump divisions; also from seed.
USES: A most useful cut flower, it fits into many arrangements.
CULTURAL HINTS: Divide the plants every other year. Feed frequently with a well-balanced fertilizer.

ROSE-MALLOW (*Hibiscus moscheutos*). Mallow Family
A European plant now naturalized from Massachusetts to Florida, and inland to the Great Lakes. Its very large flowers come abundantly in late summer. Related species are grown in Hawaii and the South Sea Islands, where one of these flowers worn behind the left ear means "I desire a lover." Worn behind the right ear it signifies

▲

"I have a lover." Behind both ears means "I have one lover and desire another."
HEIGHT: 2 to 4 feet.
COLOR: Pink, red, white.
LOCATION: Half sun, full sun.
SOIL: Rich, wet loam; naturalized in swamps and coastal marshes.
PROPAGATION: Start from clump divisions or from seed.
USES: Planted in groups it creates a spectacular showing. Can be used with shrubs.
CULTURAL HINTS: Keep well fed and keep the ground moist.

SOUTHERNWOOD; LAD'S LOVE; OLD MAN (*Artemisia abrotanum*). Composite Family
Related to our Western sagebrush; but this species is native to southern Europe and Asia. Pungent foliage. The green leaves are separated into feather-like divisions. The aromatic quality is one of its chief attractions. Grown in English gardens for more than five centuries, it was the ingredient of many an old-time love charm. Still used to keep away moths, to dye wool yellow, to relieve asthma.
HEIGHT: 2 to 3 feet.
COLOR: Yellow, white.
LOCATION: Full sun.
SOIL: Light, well-drained ordinary soil.

PROPAGATION: Seed sown in the spring, or separation of roots.

USES: To make sachets. To add a fragrant corner to the perennial bed. Does well in a seaside garden. Can make a nice low hedge.

FRAGRANT. Scented, especially when crushed.

CULTURAL HINTS: Give water ◀ frequently during the summer.

SUNFLOWER *(Helianthus sparsifolius)*. Composite Family
Native of Central America and Peru. Emblem of the Sun God. Patterns of this flower are carved on Inca temples, and Sunflowers worked in gold were worn by priests and virgins of the Sun. A tough and hardy plant, superb when grown for a massed effect. The flowers are spectacular in their height and vivid color and general showiness. In olden times people used to eat the flower buds the way we eat artichokes. The Indians of Peru cultivated this plant for its fibers; they also made a yellow dye from the flower petals.

HEIGHT: 6 to 7 feet.
COLOR: Yellow.
LOCATION: Full sun.
SOIL: Rich, limy soil.
PROPAGATION: Does well from seed; also by division of plants in the very early spring.
USES: Lends itself well to natural-

▼

izing. Effective in groups at the back of the border if space is large enough.

CULTURAL HINTS: Feed lime occasionally during the summet, also a balanced plant food. Keep reasonably moist and cultivate regularly.

KNIPHOFIA; RED-HOT POKER PLANT *(K. uvaria)*. Lily Family
The more water during growth, the redder and hotter the "pokers." A conversation piece in the garden; the flower spike is shaped like an inter-planetary rocket. Native of South Africa. Some fine horticultural varieties are grown in the Botanic Garden in Baden-Baden. Named in honor of Professor Kniphof of Erfurt, Germany, a prominent garden writer of the eighteenth century.

HEIGHT: 2 to 5 feet.
COLOR: Various tones of red, yellow and orange; some with white basal flowers.
LOCATION: Full sun.
SOIL: Sandy, well-drained soil. Does well in poor earth.
PROPAGATION: Divide the roots in the spring. Also propagate from seed.
USES: Ideally placed in front of shrubbery, where their vivid tones stand out against the quieter greenery.
CULTURAL HINTS: Keep moist. Supply a winter mulch to protect against cold.

▼

FLOWERS THAT START IN FALL AND WINTER

▲

PLUMBAGO (*Ceratostigma plumbaginoides*). Plumbago Family
Myriads of cobalt-blue flowers, interesting reddish-stemmed plant with shiny green oval leaves. Native of north China and the Himalayas. Blooms for many weeks during the fall.

HEIGHT: 6 to 9 inches, tending to trail across the ground.

COLOR: Brilliant blue.

LOCATION: Exposed sunny location.

SOIL: Adapts to every soil, but must have good drainage; will not tolerate excessive winter wetness.

PROPAGATION: Division of plants. Also starts well from seed.

USES: Makes a fine edging plant. Excellent in the front of the border. Good in rock gardens; does well in cities.

CULTURAL HINTS: Keep on the dry side. No need to cultivate. Feed only once a year in the spring. Does not show above ground until mid-May; can be interplanted with spring bulbs.

CHRISTMAS-ROSE (*Helleborus niger*). Buttercup Family
An unusual flower to grow in our Northern gardens because of its habit of blooming in winter. The single waxy flowers actually bloom in the snow and for a period of many weeks. ◄ Wants full sun in winter, dense shade in summer. The foliage is as attractive as the flowers—shiny, leathery, deeply divided and evergreen.

HEIGHT: 1 to 1½ feet, occasionally taller.

COLOR: White, pink-tinted.

LOCATION: Winter sun, summer shade.

SOIL: Rich loam, well drained.

PROPAGATION: Plants may be divided in August or September, but very carefully, for the roots are brittle. Seed sown in the early fall will give flowering plants in two or three years.

USES: Place near your front door or somewhere that you pass often so you see it readily as you come and go. The flower lasts well in bouquets.

CULTURAL HINTS: Feed well-rotted manure in the spring and summer when the new growth appears. Needs cool summers, and in our Southern states does better in the mountains.

CHRYSANTHEMUM (*C. mori-* ▶
folium) Composite Family
Originated in China, Japan, and India.
The Orientals eat the petals and
leaves of certain varieties in salads. One
of the glories of fall, these flowers
bring their autumn tints to your garden.
They come in many sizes and shapes.
Some have quilled petals, some spidery
ones, some flat ones, some long, some
short. They come single and double
and in pompons. However, the huge
late-flowering Florists' Chrysanthemums, which also belong in this
species, are too tender to use in our
gardens, so you must rely on the named
hardy kinds recommended by dealers in
garden perennials and described
in their catalogues. In Greek, the word
chrysanthemum means "golden
flower."
  HEIGHT: 1 to 4 feet.
  COLOR: Pink, red, purple, all the
tawny yellow and orange shades, white.
  LOCATION: Full sun.
  SOIL: Rich soil.
  PROPAGATION: Cuttings, division
of roots.
  USES: A fine addition to the
perennial border (but the hardy kinds
only—see above). Excellent as cut
flowers.
  FRAGRANT. Foliage and flowers
are aromatic.
  CULTURAL HINTS: Feed amply
during the summer. Stake the plants
and keep well watered. Cut back to one
foot before July 1. Shove the cuttings
three inches into the soil in the open
ground or in a five- or six-inch pot.
Keep moist. In a few weeks you will
have more rooted plants.

MISTFLOWER; HARDY- ▶
AGERATUM (*Eupatorium
coelestinum*). Composite Family
Clusters of furry blue flowers last a
week in water. Easy for beginners.
Combine beautifully with yellow
chrysanthemums in the perennial border. Native from New Jersey to Florida
and Texas.
  HEIGHT: To 2 feet.
  COLOR: Lavender-blue and dark
violet varieties.

  LOCATION: Full sun, partial shade.
  SOIL: Adapts to various soils,
but these must be well drained.
  PROPAGATION: Divide the plants
in the spring.
  USES: A fine plant for the border;
excellent for cut flowers.
  CULTURAL HINTS: Each spring
give a good application of well-rotted
manure.

WINDFLOWER; JAPANESE ▶
ANEMONE (*Anemone japonica*).
Buttercup Family
Anemos, in Greek, means wind; and
a great many kinds of this beautiful
plant do grow naturally in high mountain meadows. However, this species
is an exception; it came to our gardens
originally from Shanghai and near the
coast of China. The flowers are delightful in bouquets as well as in the garden,
where they are among the loveliest
and most graceful of perennials. They
are welcomed in the early fall, when
there isn't too great a variety of bloom,
and they sometimes continue to come
until frost.

HEIGHT: 2 to 3 feet, or higher.
COLOR: Rose, pink, white.
LOCATION: Part sun to full sun.
SOIL: Rich, moist soil that has
been worked deeply and is slightly acid.
Not averse to some clay.
PROPAGATION: From root divi-
sions made in early spring.
USES: A definite asset in the
perennial border, where they bloom
when many other flowers are finished.
Lovely with autumn crocus. Fine as
cut flowers.
CULTURAL HINTS: Keep moist
and feed several times during the
summer.

USES: Good flowers for cutting.
Popular in the perennial border.
FRAGRANT. Delightful scent.
CULTURAL HINTS: Feed with fertilizer low in nitrogen to encourage
more flowers and less foliage. Allow
plenty of space in the border, and
stake to keep upright.
▼

SALVIA (*S. sclarea*). Mint Family
The woolly silver-green leaves are distilled for a perfume and are used to
flavor some German wines. Grows
wild in Italy, and an improved, stately
variety has been developed in the
Vatican gardens. The single flowers are
an inch or more long and grow in
whorls upward on branching stems,
the effect forming pyramids of color.
HEIGHT: 3 to 4 feet.
COLOR: Lavender-pink and white;
the pink parts are actually bracts.
LOCATION: Full sun.
SOIL: Rich soil, well drained.
PROPAGATION: Start new plants
from divisions in the spring. This is a
biennial and short-lived.

▲

SALVIA (*S. pitcheri*). Mint Family
The lovely tall blue flower spires need
plenty of room in the perennial bed.
Four square feet per plant is not
too much. The foliage is gray-green; the
flowers, a soft but bright blue, bloom
in August and September. A native
plant from Minnesota to Kansas and
westward, and, of course, cultivated
and improved by nurserymen.

HEIGHT: 3 to 4 feet.

COLOR: Blue-violet, purple, white.

LOCATION: Full sun.

SOIL: Well-drained rich soil.

PROPAGATION: Start from divisions in the spring, or seed sown in
spring.

USES: Lovely in the perennial
border. The blue varieties are especially
attractive in an all-blue garden.

CULTURAL HINTS: Keep on the
dry side and feed with a plant food low
in nitrogen lest the plant run more to
foliage than to flowers. Give a winter
mulch to protect from cold. The
flower spikes tend to flop over, and
should be supported by brush or
thin sticks.

MONKSHOOD (*Aconitum fischeri*).
Buttercup Family
◄ Native to the mountains of Europe
and Asia. It is not only appealing in
the garden, but its roots are the source
of the drug aconite, useful as a heart
sedative. Each floret resembles a friar's
hood, hence the popular name. Interesting dry seedpods develop after the
blooms fade. Flowers in late August,
September and October. Effective and
interesting foliage. The leaves, seeds
and roots are violently poisonous to eat,
but not to touch, unless their juices
get into scratches.

HEIGHT: 3 to 6 feet.

COLOR: Deep purple-blue to
azure—variable.

LOCATION: Semishade.

SOIL: Rich soil.

PROPAGATION: Start from seed
sown outdoors in the spring. Also
divide the thick tuberous roots in late
fall or early spring.

USES: Beautiful in the border
with its showy flowers, leaves and
seedpods.

CULTURAL HINTS: Do not transplant. Let plants grow where you
establish them. Keep the soil fairly
moist. Stake. Feed regularly.

6. Perennials,
Their Lore and Care

The perennial is the plant that continues in the garden year after year and flowers every summer. Sow a perennial seed in the spring, and by fall you have a plant that will bloom the following season, and each one therafter, growing lovelier the longer it is established. If you buy young plants in the spring, they bloom the first summer. Perennials, if content where you set them out, are generous in their growing habits, and most kinds may be divided every two or three years. You are in this way able to enlarge your garden, start a new one, contribute amply to the garden club plant sale or to your friends' gardens. Perennials become old friends, practically family members, and are usually steady and dependable. In the spring you greet them as you clear away their winter covering of leaves. Tiny green spears perk up here, a giddy little frilled leaf there, and beyond, strange, pale buttonhooks emerge at ground level. As you kneel, clearing leaves in the newly warm spring sunlight, you are filled with anticipation—envisioning the way things will look in a few weeks, in midsummer and in the fall. There are certain perennials for each summer month and, even more desirable, a number of special ones that will bloom continuously from June to October—and some very hardy varieties even from May to frost.

When you commence growing perennials, your point of view does change, however. The foliage of a good, healthy plant becomes as interesting as the flowers it will soon produce. In many instances the seedpods, too, are equally attractive. When new to gardening, we sometimes think only in terms of flowers, and the more and the larger the better. No one will deny the pleasure gained from plenty of blossoms—but must we enjoy only the flowers? Wouldn't that be like all day and no night? In our day, in our garden, there is also the need and the beauty of the quiet time between. How appealing it is to consider the curve of a green leaf, a clump of promising buds, the various shapes and textures of seedpods as they ripen. In fact, the whole cycle from early spring through bloom, seed, and fall growth is rewarding to observe.

While an inexpensive way of acquiring a number of perennials is to raise them from seed sown in the spring for flowers one year hence, a quicker way is to buy plants for blooms the first summer. Your local nursery is an ideal source. Transported from nearby, the new plants will scarcely realize they have been moved. You can also get more specific varieties by sending to one of the large catalogue houses, which raise, in quantity, splendid assortments that are packed carefully and shipped promptly to your door.

Before ordering, of course, you must select a place where your perennial garden is to grow. Except for the semishade garden in the group of plans here, all these perennials are sun-loving. Perhaps a small garden is in your mind, possibly a mere few plants in that space by the wall, in the area just beyond the tree. Or are you more ambitious? What about that stretch at the top of the steps to the terrace? Remember, when you set out perennials you are establishing something for good. Where would you most like a thriving little garden forever, or almost forever? After all, since perennials are settling in for so long a time, they rate a solid start, a thorough welcome. If you dig and prepare your soil correctly the first year, in subsequent years all you need do is loosen the earth among them occasionally and scatter a little plant food.

After deciding on one of the beds diagrammed here, or one shaped to your own fancy, dig the area to a spade's depth, turn over the soil, and prepare as for annuals, removing roots, large stones and sod. Incorporate a good organic fertilizer in the earth. Then you are ready for the plants to arrive. If they come by mail, they will most likely arrive in damp moss. After carefully unwrapping, separate, soak, and plant them late some afternoon, spreading out the roots as they seem to grow naturally. Water again when they are in the ground. It is a safe rule to set each plant at crown level with the earth. Firm the soil so the plant is well anchored. The top growth, if any, may be pale or white from its trip in the dark. You can put baskets over these delicate shoots for a day or two until they get used to bright light. A few weeks after these perennials are established and thriving, give each one a little plant food, stirring it into the soil a few inches away from the plant. In June, apply a good mulch—a two- to three-inch layer of grass clippings, buckwheat hulls, cocoa mulch, or something similar to keep moisture in, weeds down, and to encourage the useful worms beneath to keep busy.

If some plants grow tall and unwieldy, a small green stake or two and some raffia solve the problem of their flopping over. To assure continuous bloom, keep dead flower heads picked off during the summer. Let the plant form seeds each fall.

The other care a perennial garden needs comes in autumn. After a few frosts, a layer of leaves will prevent the ground from frost heaving and loosening the roots from their source of nourishment. Often leaves will, of their own accord, drift over the plants, and nature will cover for you—in which case, merely add a few branches to hold everything in place. If the bed is near the house and you have hemlocks that need pruning, use their branches. The greenery is lovely lying on the ground all winter and occasionally breaking through the snow. In the spring, remove the leaves gradually over a period of a week or so. Begin at the end of March, and with your fingers brush them away—gently, lest you disturb delicate, pale shoots of new growth. Fortunately, this earliest growth will survive a few night frosts.

The only other need perennials have is a delightful one. Every couple of years, divide the plants. Do this when they appear to take up more than their share of room in the bed. At first you will probably use the surplus in the blank spaces in your own garden, but soon you will have extras to share. The most successful time to move and divide most perennials is early spring or early September. As a rule, the spring-blooming plants are best divided in September, and vice versa. Pick a cloudy day and lift the whole plant. If you feel carefully among the roots, usually they come apart in your hands into two or more divisions. Plant these divisions with plenty of water and, as when they were new, keep well watered for a few days. You won't have to divide again for another few years.

SEVEN GARDEN PLANS

I A Perennial Garden for Semishade

These flowers thrive in filtered sunlight along a wall or a fence or some other out-of-the-way area, perhaps near a large tree. There are 24 plants of 8 different varieties, and they bloom in succession. All have attractive foliage, even when not flowering. From May to October something will always be at its best, blooming gloriously and inviting you to stay a while and look and appreciate.

1. 2 Bleedingheart (*Dicentra spectabilis*), pink 2½ ft.
2. 5 Carpathian Harebell (*Campanula carpatica*), blue 6 in.
3. 3 Columbine (*Aquilegia*), pink, yellow, blue 2 ft.
4. 2 Evening-primrose (*Oenothera biennis*), yellow 2 ft.
5. 3 Foxglove (*Digitalis purpurea*), pink, white, yellow 3 ft.
6. 2 Mistflower (*Eupatorium coelestinum*), blue 1½ ft.
7. 2 Monkshood (*Aconitum fischeri*), blue 2 ft.
8. 5 Pansies (*Viola wittrockiana*), mixed colors 6 in.

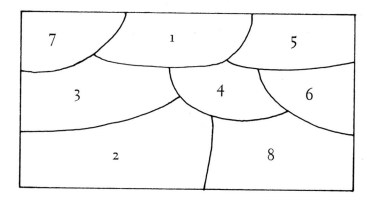

II A Perennial Corner Garden for Fragrance

Somewhere close to the living part of your outdoors, perhaps by the porch or at one end of the terrace, or near the front or back door, or where you often walk, grow this special 4-by-4-foot corner of fragrances. It contains 21 plants of 7 different varieties, all delightfully odoriferous. Here, during the whole summer, something new and different will be flowering in fascinating sequence and scenting the surrounding atmosphere.

1. 5 Carnation (*Dianthus caryophyllus*), pink, white 18 in.
2. 2 Garland Flower (*Daphne cneorum*), pink 10 in.
3. 1 Gas Plant (*Dictamnus fraxinella*), pink 2½ ft.
4. 3 Maiden Pink (*Dianthus deltoides*), pink, red, white 1 ft.
5. 2 Phlox (*P. paniculata*), white 2½ ft.
6. 5 Siberian Iris (*I. siberica*), white 2 ft.
7. 3 Siberian Wallflower (*Erysimum asperum*), yellow 1½ ft.

III A White Perennial Corner Garden
for Night Enjoyment

A special corner garden measuring 4 by 4 feet. While brilliant reds, yellows, blues fade at sundown, white stands out clear and bright. Such a plot as this, strategically located and planted with a succession of white flowers, will be a place to delight the eye at day's end. And white flowers in the moonlight have a special sheen.

1. 2 Hollyhock (*Althaea rosea*) 5 ft.
2. 2 Shasta Daisy (*Chrysanthemum maximum*) 2 ft.
3. 1 Snow-in-Summer (*Cerastium tomentosum*) 1 ft.
4. 3 Tall Bearded Iris (*I. Germanica*) 2 ft.
5. 2 Windflower (*Anemone japonica*) 2 ft.

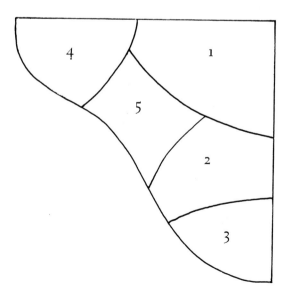

IV A Perennial Garden for a Hot Dry Spot

Seven varieties, 15 plants, in this 3-by-6-foot garden, all selected for resistance to heat and drought. The flowers thrive at the seashore as well as in semi-arid hot spots. They are hardy, and most of them bloom from early summer to late fall.

1. 2 Achillea (A. *millefolium*), white 2½ ft.
2. 2 Blanketflower *(Gaillardia aristata)*, red, yellow 2 ft.
3. 2 Sunflower *(Helianthus sparsifolius)*, yellow 6 ft.
4. 3 Sweet William *(Dianthus barbatus)*, pink, red, white 1½ ft.
5. 2 Valerian *(Centranthus ruber,* formerly V. *coccinea),* old rose 2 ft.
6. 2 Verbascum (V. *olympicum),* yellow 3 ft.
7. 2 Veronica (V. *longifolia subsessilis),* blue 2 ft.

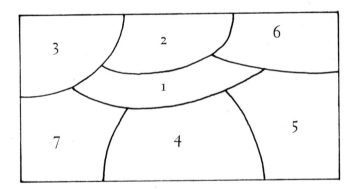

V A Corner Picking Garden of Perennials

A 4-by-6-foot garden of masses of flowers, 5 different varieties, 3 of each kind, all selected for a long blooming season, some from May to October. All these flowers are perfect for picking, as well as for sheer enjoyment as you watch them grow. Each variety is chosen for its individual loveliness and also for its happy contribution to mixed bouquets.

1. 3 Achillea (*A. millefolium*), flame 2 ft.
2. 3 Balloonflower (*Platycodon grandiflorum*), lavender 2 ft.
3. 3 Blanketflower (*Gaillardia aristata*), yellow 18 in.
4. 3 Bleedingheart (*Dicentra spectabilis*), pink 1 ft.
5. 3 Cornflower (*Centaurea montana*), blue 18 in.

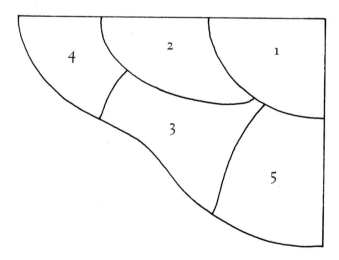

VI One of a Kind—A Perennial Garden Variety

Twelve different varieties and plants exhibit perennials at their glowing best in this 3-by-6-foot garden. The flowers were chosen for their long blooming periods; many of them flower continuously from May to October, creating a mass of color all summer long.

1. Baby's Breath (*Gypsophila paniculata*), white 2½ ft.
2. Carpathian Harebell (*Campanula carpatica*), blue 8 in.
3. Chrysanthemum (*C. morifolium*), white 3 ft.
4. Cutleaf Coneflower (*Rudbeckia laciniata*), gold 3½ ft.
5. Garland Larkspur (*Delphinium cheilanthum* 'Belladonna'), blue 3 ft.
6. Globeflower (*Trollius europaeus*), yellow 2 ft.
7. Maiden Pink (*Dianthus deltoides*), pink 1 ft.
8. Phlox (*P. paniculata*), salmon 3 ft.
9. Pincushion Flower (*Scabiosa caucasica*), lavender 2 ft.
10. Plumbago (*Ceratostigma plumbaginoides*), blue 1 ft.
11. Verbena (*V. rigida*), lavender 1 ft.
12. Veronica (*V. longifolia subsessilis*), blue 2 ft.

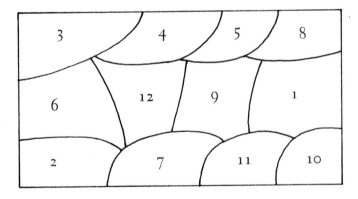

VII A Three-Primary-Color Perennial Garden

This 3-by-6-foot garden contains 3 each of 3 different varieties, making a blazing corner of red, yellow and blue from June until fall. At all times this small spot will be a place to pick countless bouquets or to feast your eyes on gay colors.

1. 3 Coreopsis (*C. grandiflora*), yellow 2½ ft.
2. 3 Garland Larkspur (*Delphinium cheilanthum*), blue 3 ft.
3. 3 Geum (*G. chiloense*), red 2 ft.

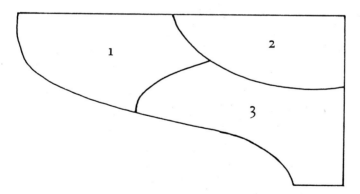

7. Grow a Primrose Path

Nothing is as completely and utterly unpredictable as gardening. I am thinking of those Primroses. It was April—with spring fever, warming soil, seed packages and three delightful Primrose plants in a grocery-store window! Large and lush and yellow they were as they caught and reflected the sunlight that golden morning. It was one of those days when anything could happen, and all of it good. Still, I never anticipated to where three Primroses could lead.

They traveled home snuggled down among the butter and carrots and a vanilla bean. The groceries are long since forgotten, but by the second season those three Primroses, planted informally in the wooded area along the brook, had doubled their size and number of blooms. Obviously they liked their environment. In England the hedgerows burgeon with flaming Primroses, which receive no special cultivation or care. Why not have an "English woods" with, not dozens, but hundreds and maybe some day even thousands, of Primroses running riot in sweeps, in clusters, and with utter abandon? Why not, indeed?

Thus, the Primrose path was born, and the Primrose path winds on and on, growing lovelier and longer each year.

A Primrose is an herbaceous perennial and a fine plant from all angles. *Primula* comes from *primus*, meaning "first," and alludes to its early bloom. The foliage, attractive at any season, has an interesting rough texture and deep, pure green color. I remember one autumn morning after the night temperature had dropped below freezing, when I stood by the bed of seedlings completely charmed by rows of little Primroses, each bright-green oval leaf picoteed in white frost.

There exist well over five hundred species of *Primula* in various parts of the world. The one I am discussing here is *P. polyanthus*, unknown in the wild state and probably descended from natural hybrids of the common *P. vulgaris* of Europe, the English Oxlip, *P. elatior*, and the fragrant yellow Cowslip, *P. veris*. This mysterious hybrid is often called Polyantha or Bunch Primrose, and comes in many colors today.

The plant itself has great character and individuality. Sometimes it simply vanishes in July and you sigh and say, "Well, it *was* a lovely spring." But lo and behold! Come late August, appealing green leaves perk up from the supposed dead center. By fall, a fine plant, completely resurrected, is ready for a winter lull and a flamboyant spring.

Primroses make a fine ground cover, having but a short winter rest. In warmer climates they remain green all year. Where winters are colder they die down in December after many hard frosts, and reappear in very early March. The flowers commence in April, and keep coming and going for nearly two months. Their colors include yellows, from rich gold to pale cream; rusts, apricot and all the tawny shades; reds, purples, and mahoganies; deep and pale blues; white. And some have contrasting eyes. While just about every rainbow color can be represented in your Primrose garden, if you wish, let the yellows predominate. For every plant of a different hue, have two or three of gold. So vivid and alive are the yellow Primroses, and so very welcome in the spring when we all, yearn for anything that suggests the bright warm sun.

Any area, any length of path, or even a simple wooded corner has in it a potential Primrose path. Whether four feet long or four hundred, it can have charm. It isn't necessarily length and size that make for success, but rather an indefinable element compounded of composition, arrangement, rightness and vigor of the plant material involved.

If possible, let the soil on your Primrose path be partly composed of rotted leaves and old stumps. Ideally, let it be rich, black and loose, and almost always slightly moist to the touch. If there is a nearby stream that runs with ample water the year around, your Primroses may occasionally be under water during the flooding spring rains. This will do them no harm. A brook isn't essential, however.

A good slope is one to the south. Primroses like morning sun or afternoon sun, and prefer to be shaded from the noonday heat. Filtered sunlight may dapple them at midday, and no harm done.

Primroses will thrive on a slope facing east, south, or west, but not so well on the north. But they definitely do want a cool, moist area. In other words, if your land is high, dry and hot, better to plant marigolds!

Let your goal for numbers of Primroses be unlimited. Each year, buy a few more from the catalogues or the local nursery, and maybe even your grocery store. (You can successfully transplant Primroses and set them out in full flower.) But in the main you may want to sow a great many seeds on your place; this is the least expensive way to extend your Primrose path. Sow some seeds in March or April indoors, more in May and June outside. The latter do equally well. It is just that in March, with spring beginning, most of us have the urge to plant something—so begin with Primroses. Most of these first-year seedlings will flower the following spring on the Primrose path—tentative small blooms, to be sure, and only a few, but enough to reveal the colors. The subsequent spring they will really let go and blossom riotously.

When icicles are stiff and glittering on the eaves of the house, you can sow the shiny black seeds indoors in flats. Use one part each of sifted leafmold, loam and sand. If you live near pine trees, scoop away the fallen needles and get a basketful of the half-decomposed material beneath. When sifted, this is an ideal mixture for seeds. Vermiculite is also fine, either plain or mixed with rich, humusy soil. Sphagnum moss is likewise satisfactory.

Sow seeds an eighth to a quarter of an inch deep. Press the soil firmly down, water with a fine spray, and keep in the shade (shading prevents sudden drying out). When seedlings first appear, bring them to the sunlight, and never let them dry out completely. What a delight to watch them grow. There is nothing more enticing than small green Primrose seedlings in early spring. You can so easily envision them blooming by the dozen where you mean them to grow in your garden.

Meanwhile, when bright green seedlings have two true leaves, separate them, after a good soak, to stand an inch apart in rows in flats, and again keep in the shade for a few days. When plants grow thick again it will be May and time to set them six inches apart outside in a nursery bed, which should have no more than five hours of sun daily. In this nursery bed you can also sow seeds in May and June. Incorporate leafmold into the top layer of well-pulverized soil, which has previously been freed of stones and earth lumps. If you are in a mood to coddle your plants, sift the top two inches of soil before planting.

When sowing directly outside, drop the seed more thinly, and do only one transplanting, to six inches apart. Let plants remain in the nursery through the following winter. Early the next spring, set them along your Primrose path.

If you have too much sunlight on your seedbed area, erect a small canopy of cheesecloth tied to fifteen-inch-high sticks over the plants. It will resemble a miniature tobacco farm; but the results are fine!

Come that first fall, cover the small thrifty plants with small pine or evergreen branches, and then leaves. The branches prevent the leaves from packing on the new crowns.

When ready to establish the young Primroses on your Primrose path, first spade up an area a bit larger than they will need for growth and elbow room. Free it from roots and encroaching greenery. A few trowelfuls of leafmold or superphosphate mixed in the soil under each plant is helpful. One of my favorite pastimes is to wander in our woods with a small dump wagon or basket collecting leafmold and material from inside old rotted stumps. Both greatly spur Primroses to their best.

In planting Primroses you will discover that they look best when set in a casual, unplanned manner. Group, say, seven in one area, staggering them nonchalantly along the way. Establish three more just there as the path turns. Then, on the opposite side, a little farther on, five more, and a baker's dozen beyond. Perhaps by that old stump, plant one in the sheltering arms of its buttressed roots. Set each plant and firm the soil up around the crown, but never cover it. Water, and then the fun begins. Observe how they take hold and begin to grow.

Maintenance of the Primrose path is practically nil in a normal season. Keep plants free from weeds and encroaching greenery. Mulch around them with old, well-rotted manure, pine needles or leafmold, all of which nurture beneficent bacteria in the soil. Water in a drought year or a prolonged dry spell. There is no need, in a wooded area, to winter cover, for nature does it well.

Plants may be divided every other year; the best moment is right after blooming. The crowns separate easily as the Primrose is lifted from the ground and gently parted by hand. Water immediately after re-setting and for a few days thereafter.

And so, when spring sweeps over the meadow, swinging catkins along the brook, when clouds race and the sun grows warmer each day, head for the Primrose path. Down across your sunny meadow, perhaps, and then you step over a low rock and into a cool place of many fragrances. The path curves a little. . . . All at once you see them and gasp— you cannot help it. Drifts of Primroses informally border the path: gold, lemon-yellow, apricot, red, and blue.

From across the meadow sounds the music of a lark as the breeze bends the wild iris foliage. A new season is fully here, coasting in on a riot of Primroses—and there on an old stump you pause a while to be part of it.

8. Six "Problem" Perennials

This is the story of six different plants and their secrets. The story of six difficult plants—but not six impossible plants. Once you know the keys to their success these six become thrilling flowers to raise. The fact that they are difficult makes it more rewarding when they do so well. Each one, in its turn during the season, becomes a dramatic accent and the true Sarah Bernhardt of the garden.

Oriental Poppies, sensational and dazzling, come in May. Fragrant Peonies and Japanese Iris large as dinner plates are for June. Tall, blue Delphinium spires bloom in early summer, and again in September. Deep blue Monkshood rings in the autumn, and waxy white Christmas-roses flourish and flower in mid-winter. These plants vary in color, height and season of bloom, but they all share "temperament." Each is a true challenge to anyone willing to accept it.

Full of hope and enthusiasm, you buy one of them. It is fine for a year, maybe, then dwindles away. How often do Delphiniums do this? Why? Sometimes you acquire Oriental Poppies, and instead of vibrant colors and flowers galore, a few weak leaves appear, maybe one flower. Maybe none. Why? And Japanese Iris? The book says "large as a dinner plate," and yours came up tiny and spindly. Why? Monkshood is supposed to be as deep blue as the Vermont rivers in autumn. But why were yours pale as a baby's blanket? And Christmas-roses—each one sent up a small, promising green leaf, but the promise was never fulfilled. You moved them to another location, and they grew even weaker! Where were the lovely waxy white flowers that were supposed to crop up all winter through snow and ice? Where, indeed?

It is all a matter of secrets—and here they are, beginning with the private life of that exotic bloom, the Poppy.

ORIENTAL POPPIES (*Papaver orientale*) grow two and a half to three feet tall. The flowers transform the garden for three weeks. Blooms eight or more inches across come in white, pink and scarlet. Poppies unfold to reveal dusty, dark stamens that tremble in the slightest zephyr. The red shades are wild and wonderful. Avoid pink or yellow neighbors for these. They are best grown apart, backed by evergreens or a weathered board fence. The white and dusty pink shades mix happily with other perennials. In midsummer the foliage withers and the plant disappears completely for six weeks. After that leaves reappear.

The special touch needed begins with planting. Select a sunny, well-drained bed filled with deep, rich loam, newly dug. Move, together with their balls of earth, in late summer. Give ample elbow room and set at least two feet apart. Instead of placing the Poppy as it grew, tip the plant to a 45-degree angle. This avoids crown rot. Cover with a three-inch layer of soil. Poppies respond to two meals during the summer of leafmold and bone meal or a general fertilizer. Water in dry spells until leaves die down; then the roots can take a summer baking. During the first winter, give a mulch of straw or grass clippings. Put the material under, never over, the foliage. Watch out for winter heaving, and in the early spring press the plants firmly back into the soil. Don't be frightened; be *firm*.

To multiply your favorite after it has become well established, transplant it every other year. You never find all the roots, so plants will continue to appear every season in the spot from which you have removed it. The plants you succeeded in moving also flower. The more orthodox way of turning a single plant into many is to dig one up in August as the new growth commences. The roots are like a bunch of white carrots. Cut every "carrot" into two-inch pieces and plant separately three inches under the soil. Be sure to set each one right side up. To remember which is the top, make a slanting cut across it, a straight cut at the base. You can root these cuttings in a pot and later transplant to the garden.

Some of the finest varieties include: 'Betty Anne'—pink, maroon center, long-lasting in arrangements; 'Watermelon'—cerise, dark center; 'Empress of India'—scarlet, dark center; 'White Queen'—white, deep purple center; 'Carousel'—snow white, border vivid red, and giddy as a circus.

PEONIES (*Paeonia*) are very satisfying. Though sometimes difficult to start, once successfully established they continue flowering for years. The huge fragrant blooms come in pink, red and white; single and double. Do try a variety. All through June the blossoms keep coming and going. The foliage, a rich, glossy green, is handsome throughout the summer and splendid in bouquets. Last year we had a large arrangement of Peony leaves in front of the fireplace. It lasted six weeks. All we did was change the water a few times and sit back in admiration.

The special touch needed begins, as usual, with planting, and the season for this is September. Flourishing plants and armfuls of flowers result from rich, well-drained soil and full sun. Dig the bed two feet deep and add plenty of leafmold and manure. Never let the "pure" manure touch the tuber. Select two-year-old stock, each tuber with three to five eyes. Plant them three feet apart, with the eyes two inches below the soil's surface. If set too deep they will never flower. After digging the bed, let the earth in the hole settle before planting lest tubers sink lower than you intend. After planting, water immediately. Mulch between Peonies and cover for the duration of the first winter.

Another essential for Peonies is plant food. Every spring give at least a half bushel of well-rotted barnyard manure or its equivalent to each plant, dug in around but not touching it. Feed bone meal in the fall. Peonies also respond to wood ashes from the fireplace and sheep manure. As first growth appears, give each Peony a support to steady it in wind and rain. A wire circle with three wire legs that shove into the ground is ideal. If you have nonblooming Peonies, feed, *feed*, and FEED, beginning as early as you can work the soil. Ours didn't flower at first; then they developed botrytis. We cut off and burned all the affected parts, then sprayed with fungicide. The botrytis disappeared. We revived them into spectacular blooms by giving them quantities of plant food. We gave each plant a bushel of manure, three pounds of bone meal, additional ashes and sheep manure. Our flowers were great. The basic keys to successful Peonies are rich soil, shallow planting and plenty of food.

Our favorite peonies are 'Festiva Maxima' (first grown in 1851)— white with streaks of crimson; 'Mary Brand'—fine red; 'Martha Bulloch' —deep, deep rose shading to delicate pink.

JAPANESE IRIS (*Iris kaempferi*) come into bloom from mid-June to mid-July. Plants grow to four feet. Blossoms are occasionally as large as nine inches across, and they last a week indoors. Colors range from deep purple through burgundy and pink to a soft blue to white with striking yellow markings.

The special touch needed involves three vital points: (1) A well-drained site is basic. (2) Soil must be acid (dig aluminum sulphate in annually) and rich in organic matter. (3) Plenty of moisture is needed through the growing and flowering season. After blooming, the soil can be drier.

Japanese Irises thrive beside a pool or stream, but do not want their roots in a puddle, nor do they flourish where water remains in winter. Unless it is a rainy spring, let water from the hose run several hours each week among the plants right up until blooming time. They do best in full sun, except in warm sections of the country, where afternoon shade is beneficial. Plant in late summer or early fall. Set the crowns two inches below the ground's surface. They flower the second season after planting. Well-rotted manure is the best fertilizer to incorporate before planting. Feed more of this early each spring. An oak-leaf mulch in winter, and even in summer, is excellent. If at any time the leaves turn yellow, you know that lime is present, and lime is as fatal as can be.

If, after a few years, the flowers appear to grow smaller and the stems shorter, divide the plants. Do this at any time after flowering to late September. Separate each large clump in two or three sections, no more, and you will have flowers the following year. Water thoroughly after dividing to stimulate root growth before autumnal frost.

There are innumerable Japanese Iris to choose from. Some of the Marhigo hybrids have the largest blossoms of all. Our favorites from this group include: 'Blue Pompon'—a deep blue; 'Jeweled Kimono'—a light, soft blue, of pure and delicate color; 'Imperial Palace'—a rich purple with flowers sometimes nine inches across; 'Frosted Pyramid'—a pure, pure white with a slightly double-petaled effect; 'Emperor's Robe'—a ruffled, violet-veined marvel on stems nearly three feet high. All these have touches of gold radiating out from the center.

DELPHINIUMS are magnificent! Grow these beauties near pale yellow daylilies, evening primroses, white phlox or pyrethrum. They also combine with madonna lilies and foxglove. They are splendid growing against a fence, superb in bouquets. Their colors range from white to light sky blue to deep ocean blue, some with touches of pink and lavender. The floret centers vary; some are light, some are black.

These aristocrats are very temperamental. One of their troubles is that they are basically native to high altitudes and cooler climates. They love mountain air and do wonderfully well on the Pacific Coast or in New England, where evenings are cool; they also thrive at the seashore. They are difficult, but not impossible, in the Midwest or any hot inland area. In the first place, it is easy to raise young plants from seed. You could begin here: Sow the seed in the spring in a wooden flat in a mixture of one third sand and two thirds good topsoil. Sow directly on the surface of the soil and cover with a thin layer of coarse sand. Do not use beach sand). Water with a fine spray. Set in a sheltered spot where it is bright but not sunny. Keep the soil barely moist, and in two weeks you will see the first sprouts. When they are big enough to move, set the young seedlings in the garden four inches apart and cover in the fall with leaves. Transplant to a permanent location the following spring. Divide these plants every three or four years to prevent overmultiplication.

The special touch needed for their success begins with location. The ideal site is a sunny bed on a north slope—this keeps the roots from baking heat. East or west are next best. Avoid a southern slope. They need plenty of space, so set each plant two feet from the next. Preferred soil is one with ample leafmold, compost, bone meal, ashes and a deep, rich loam—no clay. They must have perfect drainage, and the earth where they are to go must be dug to eighteen inches. Cut fading flowers after the first bloom is over, wait two weeks, then cultivate, water and feed. Delphiniums grow to six or eight feet, so support is needed. Since hot, baked earth discourages these plants, mulch the ground in summer to cool the roots.

Among the best to grow are the Pacific Hybrid Delphiniums, highly dramatic, and presenting a great wealth of colors to choose from. Some of the best are: Bluebird Series—a true medium blue with huge florets, touches of white in the center; King Arthur Series, including 'Blue Knight'—a dark violet with touches of black at the center, 'Galahad'—a pure white with florets sometimes three inches across, and 'Guinevere' —a pink lavender with touches of white; and Summer Sky Series—a light sky blue, with white touches. Two other excellent varieties are 'Belladonna'—light blue, and 'Bellamosum'—dark blue. These last two are lower-growing.

MONKSHOOD *(Aconitum)* florets are shaped like a helmet or a hood, hence the name. It is from this plant that the medicine aconite comes.

Monkshood colors are vivid blue, lilac and white. It grows three to six feet tall. The roots and juice are deadly poisonous to eat, so watch and caution children about this. The leaves are large and lustrous, and the flowers combine beautifully with chrysanthemums and anemones in the garden or indoors.

The special touch needed involves four points: (1) Food. These plants are prodigious feeders, need a rich soil to start, and plenty of cow manure and leafmold in the spring and again in midsummer. (2) Water is vital. Water abundantly during the growing season, soak during dry spells. (3) They must have partial shade. Monkshood will fail if grown in full sun. Thrives in a wild garden, semiwild areas or woodlands in filtered sunlight, and the high shade of deciduous trees. (4) Don't disturb. Take time and thought to give Monkshood the proper location to start and, if possible, protect from wind; then don't move again.

These plants may be readily grown from seed planted in the spring. The seed takes three weeks or more to germinate, so don't be discouraged waiting. Follow instructions for delphinium seeds.

Three satisfying varieties include: A. *sparksii*—flowers in July and August, grows to five feet, is deep blue; A. *fischeri*—also deep blue, blooms in September and October, grows two to three feet tall; A. *wilsoni*—lavender, a late-flowering variety (October), attaining a height of seven feet.

CHRISTMAS-ROSE (*Helleborus niger*) waits for the chill of winter to flaunt its waxlike flowers, which turn a delicate pink as they fade. Since it blooms from November to March, you will be picking these flowers literally in the snow. Arranged with evergreens, pine, hemlock, spruce, they make a lovely bouquet that lasts two weeks indoors. Christmas-roses bloom the third year after planting, but their rich, leathery evergreen leaves are always attractive. The plant grows to twelve inches. Set out any time from August to frost or in early spring. Set twelve inches apart.

The special touch needed relates to sun, moisture, soil. They must have sun in winter and shade in summer. Select a site among evergreens or under deciduous trees. They flourish near oaks, and will do well on the south side of a wall with a tree overhead. When possible, protect from north and west winds. Point two is moisture. If once the summer sun bakes them dry, they never fully recover. Water during the season, and especially in dry spells. Ours do wonderfully well among the evergreens in our foundation planting near the water spigot. Christmas-roses like the same soil that ferns do. Give them a rich leafmold and manure-filled loam. Decomposing leaves lying on the ground's surface, especially oak leaves, are most beneficial. Never move Christmas-roses.

Once you have learned the special needs and desires of these six prima donnas, they cease to be mysterious and ornery. No longer are they problem perennials. If it is not possible to follow every suggestion given, you may, following them in part, still have a considerable degree of success, and if you are able to proceed meticulously to fulfill all the individual requirements, you will outdo even the catalogue pictures! Given time and care, your garden will be truly sensational.

Index

Achillea, 103, 132, 133
Achillea millefolium, 103, 132, 133
Aconitum, 140
    fischeri, 125, 145
    sparksii, 145
    special care for, 144–45
    wilsoni, 145
African daisy, 19, 71
African lily, 105
African marigold, 58, 75
Agapanthus, 105
Agapanthus africanus, 105
Ageratum, 23, 66, 70
    see also Flossflower
Ageratum, hardy (Eupatorium
    coelestinum), 123
Ageratum houstonianum, 23, 70
Ajuga genevensis, 89
Allheal, 107
Althaea rosea, 116, 131
Alyssum, 78, 86
    sweet, 19
Alyssum saxatile citrinum, 86
Amaranth, globe, 37
Amaranthus caudatus, 57
Amberboa muricata, 46
Anagallis arvensis, 28
Anchusa, 91
Anchusa capensis, 79
    'Bluebird', 48
Anchusa myosotideflora, 91

Angel's trumpet, 50, 71
Anemone, Japanese, 124, 131
Anemone japonica, 124, 131
Anemone pulsitilla, 83
Annual gardens, 65–72
    easy, 66–68, 69
    flowers for, 66–68, 69–72, 78–80
    grouping for color, size, 77
    late, 66
    location, 65–66
    mulching, 78
    plans, 69–72; see also Garden
        plans, annual
    preparation for, 66
    for winter bouquets, drying, 68,
        72
    see also Annuals, self-seeding
Annual phlox, 27
Annuals, self-seeding, 76–80
    flowers recommended as, 78–80
    mulch for, 78
    sowing seed, 76–77
    thinning, 77, 78
    transplanting, 77–78
    watering, 78
    see also Annual gardens;
        individual plant names
Anoda lavateroides, 61
Anthemis nobilis, 114
Antirrhinum majus, 45, 79
Aquilegia, 87, 129